YOUR
PENSION
RIGHTS AT
DIVORCE

YOUR PENSION RIGHTS AT DIVORCE

What Women Need to Know

Revised Edition

Anne E. Moss

PENSION RIGHTS CENTER

Your Pension Rights at Divorce: What Women Need to Know
is intended to provide general information about pension rights
at divorce. It is being published with the understanding that
the Pension Rights Center is not engaged in rendering legal
services. This book should not be used as a substitute for legal
advice. Individuals with legal problems should consult a lawyer
for advice about their specific situations.

Library of Congress Cataloging-in-Publication Data

Moss, Anne E.
Your Pension Rights At Divorce/Anne E. Moss. —Rev. Ed.
Includes index.
ISBN 0-9643 990-0-8 (paper)
1. Pensions—Rights at divorce—United States. 2. Divorce—Legal rights
to pensions. 3. Women's legal rights at divorce—Division of pensions.
Library of Congress Catalog Card Number: 94-69780

ACKNOWLEDGMENTS

The Pension Rights Center wishes to thank the American Council of Life Insurance for generously underwriting the initial printing costs of both the original edition of *Your Pension Rights at Divorce* and this Revised Edition. We are also extremely grateful to the following foundations for their support of the Center's Women's Pension Project while this book was being written:

Ford Foundation
Muskiwinni Foundation
Rockefeller Family Fund
777 Fund

Your Pension Rights at Divorce was written by Anne E. Moss while she was Director of the Women's Pension Project to answer the pension questions women most often ask at divorce, and revised by her. Both editions were skillfully edited by editorial consultant Heddy F. Reid. Graphic designer Alice E. Hudders donated her extraordinary artistry to the book's design, and Barbara Johnson, the Center's Secretary, expertly and tirelessly typed countless drafts. We acknowledge their dedication, talent, and hard work with immense gratitude.

Special thanks also go to Center Administrator Ellen Matthews and Publications Manager Victoria Kanios, who ably handled the many details involved in the production of both books, and to Cindy Hounsell, current Director of the Women's Pension Project, who with humor, enthusiasm, and persistence successfully spearheaded the publication of this Revised Edition.

Finally, we acknowledge with appreciation the invaluable technical suggestions and comments on selected chapters provided by Edith Fierst, Mary Jane Yarrington, Mary Wurzel, Shirley Taft, Gill Deford, Elizabeth Thurston, and Miriam Chrisler.

"Wait a minute...you haven't said anything about the retirement plan."

TABLE OF CONTENTS

INTRODUCTION

About This Handbook

This handbook presents basic information about the pension rights of women upon divorce. It is meant to answer the questions women going through divorce most frequently ask about pensions. The book is aimed at divorcing *women* because they have been more likely than men to lose out on retirement benefits after a marriage ends.

Although major reforms in the laws over the last few years have given new pension protections to homemakers, it is still difficult, in many cases, to get information about all the new rules and regulations, and to learn what you have to do to get your share of a pension. This handbook has been written to help you educate yourself about the laws and how they affect you.

Using This Handbook

Ideally, you should read this handbook *before* you go through a divorce. It will alert you to things that can help you once legal proceedings begin.

The handbook is divided into three parts. *Part One* gives an overview of how retirement systems work. *Part Two* explains how state divorce laws can affect pension rights. *Part Three* discusses the rules of various retirement systems, explaining what they do or don't provide for former wives.

You should first read all of *Parts One* and *Two*. Then read the chapters in *Part Three* that apply to the types of pensions involved in your divorce. (For example, federal civil service or railroad retirement.)

Note: Many divorcing couples negotiate out-of-court settlements that divide up the marital assets, including pensions. Even if you don't expect to go to court, it's still important to know what the law says about pensions. This knowledge helps you and your lawyer decide what you can reasonably ask for during negotiations, and helps predict what a court might order if you and your husband can't agree. The more you know about your rights at divorce, the better you will be able to work with your lawyer to get your fair share of benefits.

☞ In this handbook, the broader term "retirement system" is often used instead of the more restrictive "pension plan." Although in many cases they are the same thing, the term "retirement system" is more inclusive.

Why You Need a Share of Your Husband's Pension

Many married women assume that their husband's pension plan will take care of both of them at retirement. But divorce can change the picture — you may lose the benefits of your husband's plan both during his lifetime and after he dies.

A wife who has worked in the home for most of her marriage is likely to have no pension of her own and not enough marketable skills or working years left to earn an adequate pension benefit. Wives who have been employed outside the home during marriage can't always depend on earning a secure retirement income, either. Working at low-paid jobs or jobs without pension plans, or taking time off to care for children, translates into meager retirement benefits for many women in their old age.

Although most women eventually receive social security, their average social security retirement benefit of about $500 a month is not enough to live on comfortably. *If you divorce, it is essential that you protect your rights to a share of your ex-husband's retirement benefits.*

Pensions Are Marital Assets

Federal and state lawmakers are beginning to recognize marriage as an economic partnership where earnings and property are acquired through the efforts of both husband and wife. If the wife has not worked outside the home, it is likely that her job of homemaker made it possible for her husband to pursue his career fully.

A pension, like wages, is part of a worker's earnings, even though there may be no right to receive the pension until retirement. Since the pension benefits accumulated during a marriage may be one of the greatest assets a couple owns, many courts will consider pensions earned during the marriage to be joint property and divide them between husband and wife when the marriage ends.

Take Steps Now to Get Your Share of the Pension

Despite many new reforms, there is no guarantee that a wife will receive a share of her ex-husband's pension. The social security system is the only retirement system that provides automatic benefits for a divorced spouse. The laws don't require that pension benefits be divided. You have to ask for a share, and see that the necessary legal steps for receiving it are taken *at the time of divorce,* even though you may not be able to actually collect until later when your ex-husband retires or dies.

Will You Get a Share of the Pension?

Your pension rights at divorce will depend on two different sets of rules: the *rules* of your husband's retirement system and the *divorce laws* of the state in which your divorce takes place.

The rules of the retirement system will tell you what benefits the court *can* give to an ex-wife, while the state divorce, or "domestic relations," laws will say what pension benefits the court *will* give to an ex-wife. This is an important distinction. The fact that a retirement system's rules *allow* state courts to divide pensions does not mean that the retirement system rules *require* courts to divide pensions.

Most retirement systems (pension plans) have rules set up under federal law.* Each retirement system is under a different set of laws. The federal "law" that affects your pension rights at divorce consists mostly of *statutes* (laws) passed by Congress.

Retirement System Rules

Some retirement systems have specific and fairly strict rules about rights at divorce, but other systems have broader and more flexible rules. The rules of the retirement system will ordinarily tell you:

- Whether the retirement system allows a divorce court to divide the pension.

- Whether the retirement system allows payment of a pension share directly to a former wife, rather than through the husband.

- Whether the retirement system allows a divorce court to award a widow's pension to a former wife.

---

* Retirement systems for state and city employees are an exception: They are set up under laws passed by state legislators or city officials.

State Divorce Laws

State divorce "laws" affecting your pension rights are mainly *statutes* passed by state legislators and *decisions* made by state divorce courts. In your state, you may find that the divorce statutes are very general and do not say much about pensions. On the other hand, there may be a number of court decisions specifically about pension matters.

The divorce laws within a state are usually the same for pensions from all retirement systems. By knowing about the state divorce laws, you can determine:

- Under what conditions the state court will divide a pension.

- How the state court will figure a former wife's pension share.

- How and when the state court will order a former wife's share to be paid.

- Whether a state court will order payment of a widow's pension to a former wife.

Keep in mind: Just because a retirement system says that a wife *may* be awarded a pension share at divorce does not mean that the divorce court *must* award a pension share. The court will divide the pension only if state law also provides for pension division. On the other hand, a divorce court usually cannot divide the pension if the retirement system does not allow division.

Some Cautions and Disclaimers

- Pension laws apply equally to both men and women. This handbook, however, often uses the words "wife" or "widow" in place of "spouse" or "survivor" because the laws discussed here are aimed primarily at providing protections for long-term homemakers, who are mostly women.

- For the sake of space, this handbook doesn't deal with every type of pension or other employee benefit that could be part of a divorce. Be sure to ask your lawyer about what other benefits you might be entitled to, such as health and life insurance, child support or children's benefits paid by your ex-husband's plan, and any other fringe benefits.

- You should also be aware that the laws, regulations, and court decisions having to do with pensions and divorce are continually changing. Be sure that your lawyer finds out whether there have been any new laws that might affect your situation in the state where you are divorcing.

- *Most important:* This handbook *is not a substitute for legal advice.* Rather, it will provide you with information and suggest questions for you to discuss with your lawyer. Only your lawyer is in a position to evaluate your whole legal situation.

PART ONE

OVERVIEW OF RETIREMENT SYSTEM RULES

PART ONE

OVERVIEW OF RETIREMENT SYSTEM RULES

The rules of your husband's retirement system, or pension plan, play an important part in determining your pension rights at divorce.* While it is rare for a retirement system to provide benefits automatically to a divorced wife, most retirement systems allow a divorce court to divide the pension. Within certain limits, most retirement systems also will pay a pension share directly to a former wife, and will pay her a benefit after the ex-husband dies. You or your lawyer will need to find out what benefits your husband's retirement system has available for divorced wives and what you need to do in order to claim those benefits.

In *Part One* you will find a list of questions that will suggest what you and your lawyer may want to ask about your husband's retirement system in order to figure out what benefits you can expect to receive. If your husband worked at more than one job during his career, you should ask these questions about all his pension plans. If your husband's retirement system is discussed in this handbook, most of these questions will be answered for you in the chapter in *Part Three* that covers his particular retirement system. Bear in mind that these are not necessarily the only questions you should ask, but they are good starting points.

Also included in *Part One* is an explanation of how retirement systems work and tips for contacting the retirement system.

---

* Although "pension plans" may be included under a larger "retirement system," *Part One* uses these terms to mean the same thing.

9

How Do Pension Plans Work?

A traditional pension plan is a fund in which money is set aside by an employer to pay benefits to employees at retirement. The money in the fund is likely to be invested in bank accounts, stocks, bonds, government securities, or real estate. Types of investments vary a great deal from plan to plan.

Most pension plans, whether they are company or government plans, are one of two main types — *defined benefit* or *defined contribution*. If you know which type of plan your husband has, it will be easier to understand how the plan works.

A *defined benefit* plan is one that promises to pay an individual a *specific benefit* at retirement. The benefit is usually based on a percentage of an employee's average earnings multiplied by his years of work under the plan. Sometimes employees are required to pay into these plans, but the employee's contributions usually do not determine the amount of the benefit he eventually receives.

The most common method of payment from a defined benefit plan is a lifetime monthly pension starting at retirement age. Some plans also pay benefits in the form of a lump sum. In a defined benefit plan, employees do not have separate "accounts" because all the money is pooled in a single fund. But the plan is still required to keep track of the amount of benefits each worker has earned.

Examples of defined benefit plans are the social security system, the railroad retirement system, the federal civil service and military retirement systems, and most large company and union pension plans.

Under a *defined contribution* plan, the employer only promises to contribute a certain amount per year to the plan for each employee, but *does not specify the benefit* the employee will receive at retirement. The contribution is usually a percentage of the worker's earnings that year.

Employees have separate accounts. Employees do not necessarily pay into a defined contribution plan; some plans require employee contributions while other plans allow employees the choice of paying.

In a defined contribution plan, the money that is paid in by employer and employee is invested by the plan. The benefit that an employee receives at retirement consists of whatever money has been paid in plus the investment earnings. Many of these plans pay benefits in the form of a lifetime pension, but they also commonly offer benefits in the form of a one-time payment or lump sum. Small companies often have defined contribution plans, such as profit-sharing plans, savings plans, and 401(k) plans. An example of a large defined contribution pension plan is TIAA-CREF (the Teachers Insurance and Annuity Association-College Retirement Equities Fund). This plan covers many college and university employees.

Questions You Need to Ask About Retirement System Rules

What Type of Pension Plan Does Your Husband Have?

- Is your husband covered by only one plan or more than one? Some employers provide several plans for each employee.

- What is the name of his pension plan? This information is especially important if his employer has more than one plan.

- Is his plan a *"defined benefit"* plan, or a *"defined contribution"* plan? (*See* page 10.)

- Are the plan rules determined mainly by federal law? by state law? or by another group of laws?

- Is your husband required to pay into his plan? Can he choose to make contributions to the plan? If yes, has he done so?

- Is he also covered by social security? (If so, it is very important for you to read *Part 3,* Chapter 1, "Social Security," page 49.)

What Benefits Will Your Husband Collect?

- If your husband is already collecting a benefit from his retirement plan, in what form is his benefit being paid? Is it being paid as a lifetime monthly pension, or in some other form?

- If he is now collecting a benefit, how much does he actually receive? Is his benefit the official amount of the pension or are deductions being made? What is being subtracted and why? (For example, there may be deductions for income taxes, life insurance, or health insurance.)

- If he is not already collecting a benefit, what is the earliest date that he could begin receiving benefits? Does he plan to retire at that time, or later?

- If your husband stopped working today, for any reason, would he still be eligible to collect a pension at retirement age?

- How will his benefit be figured? A pension is typically based on how much an employee earned and how many years he worked.

- If your husband hasn't yet started collecting his pension, how much has he earned in benefits thus far? How much can he be expected to accumulate by the time he does retire?

- What pension payment choices will he have at retirement? Can he be paid a benefit only in the form of a lifetime monthly pension, or can he choose a lump sum or payments in several installments? Can he provide a benefit for a survivor? Has he already provided a benefit for a survivor?

- Does the plan provide cost of living increases for pensions?

- Does the plan provide that an employee may temporarily or permanently lose benefits under certain circumstances? For example, a government or company pension may be temporarily suspended when a retiree goes back to work for the same employer or in the same industry. A government employee may lose benefits permanently if he is fired for serious misconduct.

What Benefits Can You Receive From Your Husband's Plan?

- If a court awards you a share of your ex-husband's pension, or if you can negotiate a share through your property settlement, would the plan agree to pay you your share *directly* (if the court or property settlement provided for it), or would the money have to be paid by your ex-husband?

- What is the maximum amount of your ex-husband's benefits the plan would permit you to receive? (*Note:* Keep in mind that your own state divorce law may restrict the amount you can receive even if the plan does not.)

- Does the plan say that payment to you can be made only in a certain form? (For example, must you accept your share in the way your ex-husband is paid, such as month by month?) Can your benefits start only at a certain time, such as when your ex-husband retires?

- Once you obtain a court order providing you a pension share, to which plan official or office do you send it? Do you have to send the plan other documents or information with the order?

- Does the plan have any special rules about what information must be contained in your court order? For instance, does the order need to say when your pension share starts and stops being paid?

- If you are to receive your share of the pension from your ex-husband rather than the plan, what can you do if he stops paying his share? Will the plan allow you to "garnish" his pension? (*See* "Garnishment," page 40.)

- Would your remarriage affect your share of the pension? Would his remarriage have any effect?

- Will your pension share stop if your ex-husband dies before you do? (*See* below.)

What Benefits Can You Receive After Your Husband Dies?

- If your ex-husband dies before you, will the plan pay a widow's pension to a *divorced* wife? Is a widow's pension payable only in certain situations, such as when the divorce occurs before the ex-husband's retirement?

- If a widow's pension is payable to a divorced wife, can you get this benefit if your ex-husband dies while he's still working? What if he dies after he stops working under his current plan, but before he starts collecting his pension?

- If he is already collecting his pension, did he choose a form of benefit that would provide a pension or other benefit to a survivor after his death? This is sometimes called a *"survivor option."* (A retiree is often required to take a cut in his own pension in order to provide a benefit for a survivor.)

- If your husband did choose a survivor option, are you the person he selected to receive these benefits after his death? Can you still be eligible for the widow's pension once you are divorced? What do you have to do to make sure your widow's pension *is* protected? (Chances are you will need a court order that specifies you are to receive this benefit.)

- Will the plan obey a court order requiring that you be paid a widow's pension? Or can this benefit be provided after divorce only if your ex-husband chooses to provide it?

- If your husband is already retired, but didn't choose a survivor option, will the plan let him change his mind now?

- If a widow's pension or other benefit is available to you after divorce, in what form will payment be made? That is, will you get a lifetime monthly pension or some other form of benefit, such as a lump sum? Will you have a choice?

- How much is the widow's pension? Is it based on a certain percentage of the retiree's benefit, such as 50 percent or 55 percent?

- Is the widow's pension payable to you regardless of your or your ex-husband's age when he dies? Will it start being paid immediately after his death, or only at some later date, such as the year in which he would have reached retirement age?

- Does the plan give cost of living increases to widows' pensions?

- Will your benefit be affected if you remarry? If you lose your widow's pension rights because of your remarriage, can you start collecting benefits again if your later marriage ends?

Getting Information

- Does the plan have available a booklet for employees that summarizes the plan rules? Can you or your lawyer get a copy of this booklet?

- If your husband is not yet collecting benefits, does the plan give out "individual benefit statements" to employees? Does your husband have a recent statement? The statement is likely to tell you how much in benefits he has earned thus far.

- Who runs the plan? Where is the retirement board or administrator located? Can you obtain information from that office? Do you have to have your husband's written consent or a court order before the plan will release information to you?

- Do you know your husband's social security number? Nearly every retirement system uses an employee's social security number for identification purposes.

Tips for Contacting the Pension Plan

- Make sure any letter or paper you send to the plan or retirement system contains identifying information, such as your ex-husband's name and social security number, or other information the plan will need to have in order to know whose pension you are asking about. Remember that large plans, especially government plans, may handle thousands or even millions of documents each year. Even if it is correctly addressed and identified, your letter will often go through many hands before it gets to the right person.

- Whenever you send a copy of your court order or other important documents to the pension plan, it is a good idea to use certified mail, return receipt requested.

- Always keep a copy of letters or documents you send to the plan.

- If you talk to plan officials by phone, be sure to write down the name of the person you talked to, that person's title and office or department, what you discussed, and the date of your call. Keep these records together in case you need to refer to them later.

PART TWO

STATE DIVORCE LAW AND YOUR PENSION RIGHTS:

QUESTIONS YOU NEED TO ANSWER

PART TWO

STATE DIVORCE LAW AND YOUR PENSION RIGHTS:

QUESTIONS YOU NEED TO ANSWER

Introduction

O nce you know what benefits your husband's retirement system *allows* you to receive, then you need to find out whether your state divorce court is likely to award all or part of those benefits to you. *Part Two* of this handbook discusses the pension issues most likely to come up under state divorce laws. Remember: As explained in the Introduction, state divorce "laws" (also called "domestic relations laws") include state *statutes* and state divorce court *decisions*. *State laws on pension rights at divorce are usually the same for pensions from all retirement systems.*

Because state divorce laws on pensions are still developing, you may discover that your state courts and legislators haven't answered every question about dividing pensions. In these situations, your lawyer will need to help you decide what your best options are, sometimes on the basis of an educated guess about what a court would be likely to say if it were deciding your case.

The lack of precise rules about dividing pensions may at times turn out to be a good thing for a divorcing wife, because it can allow you the flexibility to negotiate the pension-sharing arrangement that is best for your own situation. This part of the handbook points out the advantages and disadvantages of different ways of pension splitting that may be available to you.

It is also intended to help you understand what you are getting in your divorce settlement and how to protect your benefits, so that you will not be surprised or disappointed years later by not receiving the benefits you assumed you would have.

Marital Property Versus *Alimony*

The rules for awarding *marital property* and *alimony* at divorce are based on state law and therefore vary from state to state. In general:

Marital property (in some states called "community property") means an asset such as a pension, house, car, or furniture, that was earned, or bought with wages that were earned by the husband or wife during the marriage. Once the marital property is divided and the divorce becomes final, a court is not likely to change the division. A share of a monthly pension paid as marital property to a former wife usually does not stop if she remarries.

Alimony usually means monthly support payments (or sometimes, a lump sum) paid by one spouse to the other "dependent" spouse. Often called "maintenance" or "spousal support," alimony is based on the ex-wife's financial need and the ex-husband's ability to pay, and may be modified after the divorce if either spouse's financial circumstances change. Alimony can be paid for a certain number of years or for as long as the ex-wife lives, but usually stops if she remarries.

Most of *Part Two* talks about getting a share of the pension as *marital property*, rather than as *alimony*. This is because divorce courts are more likely to award a pension share as marital property than as alimony.

But if you and your husband are negotiating your own property settlement or agreement, ask your lawyer whether you would be better off arranging to receive part of the pension as alimony. Your husband may agree more readily to give you a pension share as alimony, since this could make him eligible for certain alimony tax deductions. Also, your right to a pension share may be more protected if it is paid as alimony rather than marital property if your husband later falls behind on his payments to you or declares bankruptcy.

Does Your State Law Treat Pensions as Marital Property?

Some states treat all pensions as marital property, while other states treat only some pensions as marital property. However, even if the benefits *are* marital property, a court may not actually divide the pension. Instead, it might give you other marital property of the same value as your share of the pension.

The chances are that a court *won't* treat the pension as marital property and won't divide it if you were not married to your husband at any time while he was working under his pension plan.

A wife has the best chance of receiving a pension share during her ex-husband's lifetime if, at the time of divorce, he has retired and is already collecting his pension, or if he is at least eligible to retire and start getting his pension immediately. Many state courts will also divide a future pension if the husband has worked long enough to earn the right to receive a pension (or "vest" in the pension), even if he isn't eligible to collect benefits right away. A smaller but increasing number of courts now consider a pension to be marital property and will divide it even if the husband hasn't been on the job long enough to earn a pension.

If a court does not want to treat the pension as marital property, it may still consider the fact that the husband is entitled to a pension when determining how much alimony he can afford to pay.

Courts usually will not treat the same pension both as marital property *and* a resource for alimony or support payments.

Disability Benefits

Getting a share of your ex-husband's benefits awarded to you as marital property may be more difficult if he receives a disability retirement benefit, disability insurance benefit, or workers' compensation. (Workers' compensation is a type of benefit paid to a person who has a job-related illness or injury.) A court that typically treats *retirement* benefits as marital property may say that *disability* benefits are the worker's separate property.

A regular (that is, nondisability) retirement benefit can be marital property because it represents "deferred compensation" from employment during the marriage, that is, part of his wages that were set aside for retirement benefits. A disability benefit, on the other hand, is not usually considered by the courts to be deferred compensation, but the courts may still classify it as marital property. To make this decision, the court may look to see what the disability benefit is designed to do.

A disability benefit often has more than one purpose and therefore may be treated as part marital and part nonmarital property.

The court is *more* likely to treat the disability benefit as marital property if it is meant to:

- *Compensate the Worker for Medical Expenses That Arise During the Marriage.* The reimbursement for the couple's medical expenses during the marriage is marital property.

- *Replace a Retirement Benefit the Worker Would Otherwise Have Received.* The part of the disability benefit that replaces retirement benefits earned during the marriage can be treated as marital property. When an employer offers both retirement and disability benefits, the disability benefits are often larger or payable earlier than the retirement benefits. The part of the disability benefits over and above the amount of retirement benefits earned during marriage would then be treated as the worker's separate property.

The court is *less* likely to treat the disability pension as marital property if the benefit is meant to:

- *Replace the Worker's Future Wages Lost as a Result of the Disability.* Earnings after divorce are usually not marital property.

- *Compensate the Worker for His Own Pain and Suffering, or for a Specific Illness or Injury.* These are considered to be the worker's personal losses or impairments.

In some states, the law says that a disability benefit is *never* marital property. But this doesn't mean that you necessarily lose out entirely. If your husband is receiving a disability benefit that replaces a pension or retirement benefit, the court may agree to consider as marital property the *value of the retirement benefit* that is being replaced.

How Can You Find Out How Much the Pension Is Worth?

If the pension will be treated as a marital asset, it is important for you to know what the pension is worth. Most pensions are paid monthly over the worker's lifetime, and start at retirement age. The amount a husband is to receive generally depends on how many years he worked, how much he earned, how old he is when he retires, and how long a person his age is expected to live after retirement. For example, a pension of $1500 a month payable to a retiree who is now 65 years old might be considered to have a lump sum value of $130,000.

Even though he may collect his benefit as a monthly pension, you may need to know the *"lump sum value"* (sometimes known as "present value") of the pension today if you think you might want to trade off your share for other marital property of the same value. Some courts require pensions to be valued.

Whose Money Counts?

Occasionally, a court will say that a pension is worth no more than the amount of the *employee*'s own contributions, that is, the funds that were actually deducted from each paycheck. This means that if the *employer* put money into the pension plan for the employee, that money won't be counted in valuing the benefits. The problem with this approach is that in a number of retirement systems, such as the military retirement system and many state and local government plans, *only* the employer pays in. Similarly, in most private company plans, only the employer pays in. Even when the employee does pay in something, the employer usually pays in much more. In such cases, your lawyer may want to try to persuade the court that both employee *and* employer contributions should be counted in valuing the pension.

How Is Your Share of the Pension Figured?

You are not automatically entitled to a certain amount of a pension. A former wife's share is usually determined by negotiations between the spouses or their lawyers or, if negotiations are unsuccessful, by the courts. There are several steps in figuring your share.

What you will receive may depend, in part, on whether the pension can be considered marital property under state law. Most courts say that only "marital property" can be divided at divorce. Property that is not marital is "separate property."

In some states, the courts will also award a portion of one spouse's separate property to the other spouse, if needed for a fair division of assets. In still other states, the law treats as divisible just about all the property that both spouses own at the time of divorce, no matter when it was acquired. But in deciding what is your share, the court may still take into account whether the pension was earned during the marriage.

What Part of the Pension Counts as Marital Property?

Most often, only the pension benefits accumulated during your marriage count as marital property. If you and your husband were married during all the time that he worked under the pension plan, then the *entire* pension would normally be marital property. But if you were married for only part of your husband's career under his pension plan, then only *that part* of his benefits is marital property.

When Is the Marriage "Over"?

State divorce laws have different rules about when marital property *stops* accumulating. Some states say that marital property is the property that accumulates from the date of your marriage up to the date when the husband or wife moves out of the family home or files for divorce. Other states might say that it stops accumulating only when the divorce becomes final. You will need to find out what the state where you are divorcing says about when your marriage ends.

Ways of Figuring Marital Property: The Time Rule Method

This section is intended to give you a rough idea of how courts and lawyers decide how much of the pension is marital property and how they figure your share of that amount.

There are a number of different ways of figuring the marital property portion of the pension. Explained here is the "*time rule*," one of the simpler methods often used by courts and lawyers negotiating property settlements. You will see how the rule can be used in different situations.

Generally, the time rule method says that the marital property portion of the pension is equal to a certain fraction of your husband's pension benefit. The top number in the fraction is the number of years your husband worked under the plan during your marriage. The bottom number is the total number of years your husband worked (or will work) under the plan. Your share comes out of that fraction.

Note: To keep it simple, the numbers in these examples assume that the marital property portion of the pension goes from the date of marriage up to the date of divorce, and that the wife's share will be 50 percent of the "marital property," which may be less than 50 percent of the whole pension. *Your own case may be decided under different rules.*

Here's how this formula might be applied by the court, or used in your property settlement, to give you a *dollar amount* of the pension.

Dollar Amount

John has earned a pension of $200 a month by working 20 years for his company. Jane was married to him for 16 of those 20 years. Therefore, the marital property portion is 16/20 of the pension. The court decides she is entitled to half of the part of the pension that was earned during the marriage. This means she will be entitled to 50 percent of

16/20 of his pension of $200 a month. The formula would be:

■ Example 1: Jane's share of the monthly pension as a *dollar amount.*

$$50\% \quad \times \quad \frac{\text{Number of years married while John worked under pension plan}}{\text{Total number of years worked under the plan}} \quad \times \quad \text{John's monthly pension} \quad = \quad \text{Jane's share}$$

$$50\% \quad \times \quad \left\{ \quad \frac{16}{20} \quad \times \quad \$200 \quad \right\} \quad = \quad \text{Jane's share}$$

$$50\% \quad \times \quad \$160 \quad = \quad \$80$$

The marital property portion of the pension is $160. Fifty percent of that amount, Jane's share, is $80 a month.

In this example, the husband had already stopped working under his plan and therefore knew the total number of years worked. He also knew exactly how much his pension benefit would be.

The same method can be used to figure Jane's share of a lump sum. Let's say the total lump sum value of John's pension is $10,000. Jane's share of the lump sum would be $4000. The formula would be:

■ Example 2: Jane's share of a lump sum as a *dollar amount.*

$$50\% \quad \times \quad \left(\frac{16}{20} \times \$10,000 \right) \quad = \quad \text{Jane's share}$$

$$50\% \quad \times \quad \$8000 \quad = \quad \$4000$$

Percentage

Sometimes a court will specify that you will get a certain percentage of the pension rather than a specific dollar amount. This is especially likely if your husband won't be collecting his pension until years later, or if there is a chance his benefit will increase after the divorce. By using a percentage, the court doesn't have to know exactly what the pension benefit will be. In Jane's case, the formula would be:

■ Example 3: Jane's share of the monthly pension as a *percentage*.

(50% x 16/20)	x	John's pension	=	Jane's share
(50% x 80%)	x	John's pension	=	Jane's share
40%	x	John's pension	=	Jane's share

Fifty percent of 16/20 (or 80 percent) is 40 percent. Therefore, Jane will get 40 percent of John's pension, whatever the amount. The dollar amount of her share will increase if his benefit goes up. In the same way her share would also go down if his benefit decreases or turns out to be less than expected.

Percentage As of a Certain Date

A court could purposely limit your share by specifying that you get a percentage of the pension earned only as of a certain date, such as the date of divorce. This means that the amount you receive will *not* increase after divorce even if your ex-husband's benefits increase. A court would be more likely to use this formula if your husband is not yet scheduled to receive his pension because he is still working at the time you divorce. The court might say that Jane's share is:

■ Example 4: Jane's share of the monthly pension earned *as of a certain date*.

"40% of John's monthly pension earned as of the date of the couple's divorce"

Dollar Amount Plus Percentage Increase

The court could protect Jane against a possible decrease in John's benefits by using a combination of the exact dollar and percentage formulas. It could say that her monthly share is:

■ Example 5: Jane's share of a monthly pension as a dollar amount *plus a percentage of the increase.*

"$80 plus 40% of any future increase in John's pension"

In this way she will be assured of getting *no less than* $80, but she will also be able to share in benefit increases. (This helps protect Jane against any actions of John that might reduce her pension.) Another version of this formula might be:

"$80 plus 40% of future cost of living increases in John's pension"

This formula would give Jane a portion of the cost of living increases that John might receive after retirement, but none of the increases he might receive due to his additional work or raises in salary.

Future Pensions

In cases where the divorce occurs while the husband is still working, the *total number of years worked under the plan* isn't yet known and neither is the amount of the pension benefit.

A court might decide to go ahead and figure your share as shown in *Example 1* by using only the number of years your ex-husband had already worked under the plan and only the amount of his pension benefit already earned.

Another approach would be for the court to assume that the husband will work until he is first eligible to start collecting his pension. For example, if John needed to work another five years in order to be eligible to retire, instead of calculating with the 20 years he had already worked, the court would use 25 years, the number of years of work he would have at retirement age. In that case, the court could have used the estimated pension amount that John would have at retirement, based on 25 years of work. Let's say his estimated benefit would be $300 a month at retirement age. The formula would be:

■ Example 6: Jane's share of the *estimated future* monthly pension as a *dollar amount*.

$$(50\% \text{ x } 16/25) \quad \text{x} \quad \$300 \quad = \quad \text{Jane's share}$$

$$(50\% \text{ x } 64\%) \quad \text{x} \quad \$300 \quad = \quad \text{Jane's share}$$

$$32\% \quad \text{x} \quad \$300 \quad = \quad \$96$$

Jane's share of John's future pension would be $96.

Delayed Calculation

Sometimes courts prefer not to make so many guesses in order to figure a future pension share. Instead, the divorce court could issue an order that provides you a share of benefits, but doesn't give the exact amount. The court order would only show the formula to be used. Your exact share would not be figured until later. The formula would be:

■ Example 7: Jane's share of the *future* monthly pension *to be figured at John's retirement*.

$$50\% \text{ x } \frac{16}{\text{Total number of years worked under the plan}} \text{ x } \begin{array}{c}\text{John's pension} \\ \text{at retirement}\end{array} = \begin{array}{c}\text{Jane's} \\ \text{share}\end{array}$$

Jane's exact share would be figured once John started collecting his pension. If your court order or property settlement requires the plan to pay your share directly to you, then the order can say that when your husband starts collecting his pension, plan officials will figure your share according to the formula in the court order. Your lawyer should check with the plan first to make sure that this type of court order will be accepted by plan officials.

Disadvantages of the Time Rule

Although the time rule is a popular method of figuring marital property, critics say that its use may be unfair. It assumes that every year is worth the same in pension benefits; that is, it assumes that benefits increase by the same amount in each year under the plan. In fact, most retirement systems are designed so that the worker accumulates fairly small benefits in the earlier years of employment. Then benefits start to accumulate at a much greater rate once the worker has been on the job a number of years, begins receiving a larger salary, or gets close to retirement age. For this reason, your lawyer may want to use a different method of figuring the marital property portion of the pension if you were married only during the later years of your husband's work under his pension plan when he was earning better benefits.

As you can see, the best method of figuring your pension share depends very much on your particular situation. There isn't a single formula that can or should be used in every case, unless your state's divorce law requires a certain formula. Your lawyer should be able to help you decide the best way to calculate your share.

IMPORTANT: These examples are *not* meant to show how your court order or property settlement should be written to give you a pension share paid directly from the retirement system. Although a court order or a property settlement may describe the formula for figuring your share, the wording used will need to be more detailed than these examples and should follow the special rules that the retirement system may have for writing court orders. For instance, the retirement system may have a different name for the pension, such as "annuity" or "retired pay." Be sure to read the chapter in *Part Three* of this handbook about the retirement system involved in your case.

What Is Your Fair Share of the Marital Property?

If you plan to ask for a share of your ex-husband's pension as marital property, you need to know that courts, even within the same state, may award pension shares differently from case to case. Courts usually divide pensions and other assets "equitably," according to what that court believes is fair. But "equitably" is not necessarily "equally."

For example, if a woman is older, has been married for a long time, lacks the job skills and education to support herself, and has no pension, the court may award her more of her ex-husband's pension than if she is younger, well-educated, has job skills, or has a pension of her own.

In contrast, courts in California, New Mexico, and Louisiana routinely divide in half pensions and other property earned during the marriage. But unless you are divorcing in one of these states, don't just assume you should settle for half. In other states, the law says that the marital property is to be divided in half, unless husband or wife can show the court that a 50-50 division would be unfair. For example, you may be able to persuade the court to give you more than half the pension if you have been married a long time and have not worked outside the home, and there is not much other property to share in.

If husband and wife have both earned pensions, the court may award each spouse a share of the other spouse's pension, or, if the pensions are about the same size, the court may just award each his and her own pension. If one pension is larger, the couple may agree that the spouse with the smaller pension also receive half the difference between the two pensions. For example, if the husband's pension is worth a total of $50,000 and the wife's pension is worth $40,000, the wife might receive all of her own $40,000 pension plus $5,000 from the husband's pension. Each spouse will end up with $45,000 in pension benefits.

Before or After Deductions: What Are You Getting a Share Of?

The benefit amount your ex-husband actually receives is likely to be less than the official amount of his pension because taxes and insurance payments are often taken out of a pension before it is paid.

If you are to receive a percentage or fraction of the pension each month, you should know what will be deducted from that pension and whether the deductions are meant to affect the amount of your share. If your benefits are not supposed to be affected by your ex-husband's deductions, then your court order should say so. Your court order or property settlement needs to be very clear about whether your share is based on a pension amount figured *before* or *after* these common deductions:

- *Federal and State Income Taxes.* Most pensions are taxable. A retiree may normally choose to have income taxes withheld by the plan instead of paying the taxes himself. Your pension share may be less than you expected if your ex-husband has excessive amounts of taxes withheld.

- *Health and Life Insurance Premiums.* A retiree who continues to be covered by employer-sponsored health or life insurance may be paying for those benefits through a pension deduction.

- *Survivor's Pension.* Providing a widow's pension for a current or former wife usually requires the retiree to take a reduction in his own pension.

Court orders often use the words *"gross pension"* to mean the official amount specified by the plan, and *"net pension"* to mean the benefit that the retiree actually receives after deductions. However, these terms don't always mean the same thing to everyone. *Your lawyer should make sure that your court order uses wording that is absolutely clear to you, your husband, and plan officials.*

How Is Your Share Paid?

Once you have an idea how much your pension share might be, you and your lawyer will need to decide what the best way is for you to receive your share. Although both the rules of the retirement system and state divorce law may have some restrictions, you will need to make a number of decisions about the method and timing of payment of your pension share.

A Pension Share or Other Property?

Would you be better off with a share of the pension itself, or should you accept other marital property or cash equal to the value of your share of the pension? As an example, in some cases, the wife might want to agree to accept the family home rather than any part of the pension. In other cases, the law may say that the court has no power to give you a share of the pension itself, and can only give you other property or alimony. But if you have a choice and you are considering trading off your pension share, be sure to consider what other income you will have to live on during your retirement.

Who Will Pay?

If you decide to take a share of the pension rather than trading it off, do you want the pension benefits to be paid by your ex-husband or by the retirement system? (As noted in *Part One,* many retirement systems will send a pension share directly to the former wife if provided in a court order.) The advantage in collecting directly from the retirement system is that you might receive your benefits on a more regular basis. Benefits could be delayed if you have to wait for your ex-husband to send you a check each month after he gets his own check. Direct payment from the plan also protects you if your former husband should move out of state or out of the country. In addition, if your ex-husband should declare bankruptcy, you may have a better chance of preserving benefits paid to you by the retirement system.

Just keep in mind that retirement system rules for getting direct payment usually require a carefully written court order or property settlement that meets a number of technical requirements. This can mean your lawyer will be spending more time and effort on your case, costing you more money.

Payment Now or Later?

Will you get your pension share starting right after the divorce or will you get it later? Your payments might be delayed until your husband retires, or the court might not even make a *decision* about dividing the pension until after you are divorced.

Many couples, and a number of courts, prefer to see all the marital assets divided and paid out right away. The idea is that the couple will be really "divorced" and can then go their separate ways. Even if you cannot get your entire pension share out of the plan at the time of divorce (because, for example, your ex-husband has not yet retired, or his plan doesn't pay lump sums), the court might decide to award you other marital property equal to the value of your share of the pension.

On the other hand, you may be forced to wait until your ex-husband retires if the court, state divorce law, or the retirement system says that a pension share cannot be paid to a former wife until the worker starts collecting his benefits. The court order or property settlement issued when you are divorced can provide that you get a certain share of the pension starting whenever your ex-husband retires and collects his own benefits. For example, the court might say that your share will be paid to you "if, as, and when" your ex-husband receives his pension.

Rather than issuing an order at the time of your divorce, the court might instead *"reserve jurisdiction"* over the case, that is, agree to decide part of the case later, so that you and your ex-husband would have to come back when he's ready to retire to let the court figure the exact amount of your share and decide what form of benefit you are to receive (such as monthly benefit or lump sum). Having to wait to get your pension share might actually turn out to be a good thing, as you might then be able to share in any increase in his benefits since the divorce.

Your husband's retirement date isn't the only factor that can lead to delayed payment of your pension share. In some states, one or both spouses may ask the court to grant the divorce right away but leave the property division issues, including who gets the pension, to be decided later. This legal proceeding is sometimes called a "bifurcated" divorce.

One caution: If you will not be getting your pension share right away, make sure that your lawyer finds out in advance of the divorce how your pension rights could be affected if your husband remarries or dies during the period after the divorce is granted but before payment is scheduled to begin. Remember that the pension rights of a divorced wife generally depend on the terms of a court-ordered property division or a property settlement. His death, for example, could mean you would lose all claim on the pension unless you had been awarded a widow's pension in a court order or property settlement.

If your divorce decree says nothing specific about starting payments, which would be true of a "reserved-jurisdiction" or "bifurcated" divorce, then you also need to be concerned about what happens if your ex-husband retires and starts collecting his benefits or dies *before* the court gets a chance to say anything about your pension rights. One thing you might be able to do when you divorce is have a written agreement with him that he will not take any actions that might harm your future rights, such as applying for his pension, before the court has decided how the pension is to be finally divided. You should also consider getting a temporary court order providing for a survivor pension in case your husband dies before a final court order is issued.

Here is an example of what could go wrong if you don't have a court order or other agreement to protect your rights: Soon after the divorce, your ex-husband could leave his company and apply for his pension. As a single retiree, he would be free to withdraw his pension in any way the company permitted, which might include a lump sum. This would mean that he could get all his benefits out of the plan before you had a chance to claim your share.

Monthly Benefit or Lump Sum?

Once you know when you are to be paid, the next question is how, and in what form, you will collect your benefits. A typical method would be to collect your share monthly as the benefits are paid to your ex-husband. Your benefits start and stop when your ex-husband's benefits start and stop.

If your ex-husband's plan or retirement system offers lump sum payments, you may be able to collect your own benefits as a lump sum. If the plan doesn't offer a lump sum, an alternative might be for your ex-husband to pay you the lump sum *value* of your share of the pension in installments out of his monthly pension. For example, if your share of the pension is worth a total of $40,000, the court could order your husband to pay you $1000 a month from his pension until a total of $40,000, plus interest, has been paid out to you.

What Happens to Your Benefits After Your Ex-husband Dies?

Many divorced women have wrongly assumed that a pension share continues being paid for as long as they live. These women discovered, too late, that their benefits were payable only for the lives of their ex-husbands. To guard against an unexpected loss of benefits, be sure to ask your lawyer what would happen to your pension share if your ex-husband dies before you. What if he dies *before* starting to collect his pension? *After* he starts to collect?

One solution is for your property settlement to include a provision for a widow's pension. State divorce laws usually allow a couple to provide a widow's pension or other survivor benefit for the former spouse, and retirement system rules often permit the payment of a widow's pension after divorce.

Another possibility would be for your former husband to set up a life insurance policy that names you as beneficiary. If you agree to this arrangement, make sure the insurance is going to be fully paid by him and that you will remain as beneficiary even if he remarries.

IMPORTANT: Some life insurance programs provided through the federal government allow employees and retirees to drop coverage or change the beneficiary at any time, no matter what their property settlement provides.

There are other ways to ensure that your retirement income lasts as long as you do. If a private pension is involved, it may be possible to have your share of the pension paid over your lifetime. (*See* page 74.) Or, if you receive your entire share of the pension at once, you may be able to invest it to provide lifetime income.

What Is Your Fair Share of the Widow's Pension?

Even if you are to receive half of the retiree's pension during his life, you may want to ask for most or all of the widow's pension. Under many pension plans, the basic widow's pension is already reduced to about half the retiree's pension, since this survivor benefit is for one person, that is, the widow. In other words, if the retiree's benefit is $1000 a month, the maximum widow's pension is likely to be about $500 a month. If you are to receive half the retiree's pension (or $500) during his lifetime, then you should ask for the entire widow's pension to ensure that your retirement income stays the same after your ex-husband's death. If you get only half the widow's pension, your pension benefits will drop from $500 to $250 (half of $500) when he dies.

Will Taxes Affect Your Benefits?

A pension is usually taxable income and you will probably be taxed on your share. Whether you receive a share of the pension or other property in exchange for the pension, the form of benefit you receive and when you are paid will make a difference in the amount of taxes you and your ex-husband will each have to pay. *The general rule is that a divorced spouse is usually taxed on her pension share in the same way that a retired worker would be taxed.*

It is important to find out how your taxes will be affected before the court rules on your pension rights or you agree to a property settlement involving the pension. Some courts require the husband and wife to find out this tax information before the court will make a decision on the pension division. This is most likely to happen if you will be getting your pension share soon after your divorce. If you won't be receiving your share for a number of years, the court may feel that the tax information is not needed since the tax laws could change before you collect.

If You Have Trouble Collecting Your Share: Garnishment

If your former husband stops paying court-ordered support, or fails to turn over your share of the pension as ordered, you may be able to force his pension plan to pay you what is owed. This is done by a legal procedure often called "*garnishment*" or "*attachment*." Federal law specifically permits certain retirement benefits to be garnished when alimony or support payments are overdue. These benefits include social security, railroad retirement benefits, federal civil service retirement, military retired pay, private pensions, and federal workers' compensation. Even though state and local government pension plans are not regulated by the federal government, benefits from these plans can often be garnished if your ex-husband fails to pay court-ordered support or fails to pay your pension share as ordered.

Typically, you would need to have your lawyer ask a state domestic relations court to issue a garnishment order. State law usually has rules about when a garnishment order may be issued. Both state *and* federal law have restrictions on collecting the overdue amount, the types of benefits you can get access to, how soon you can collect, and how much you can collect. Federal law spells out how your garnishment order must be written before it can be used to get benefits from private pension plans and the various federal retirement systems. Some state and local retirement systems also have special rules on enforcing garnishment orders.

Your lawyer would need to find out the rules for garnishment that apply to your situation.

After The Divorce: Is It Too Late to Get Your Share?

In most cases, a wife who expects to share in her ex-husband's pension must be awarded benefits at the same time the court divides up the other marital assets (unless the court "reserves jurisdiction" so that you can come back later to claim a pension share). But many divorced women have ended up without a pension share because they didn't know their husband had a pension, their lawyer did not bring up the matter of pension rights, or they didn't know that a pension could be a marital asset.

If you only become aware of your pension rights after your divorce, can you still get a share? Most often, the answer is no. Getting a pension share nearly always requires some sort of court order or legal action that you take against your former husband. Once the divorce and property division become final, courts are usually reluctant to let husband or wife bring before the court new matters that could or should have been decided at the time of divorce.

But some ex-wives have been able to win pension benefits years later. Your success will depend mainly on what happened to the pension at divorce and what your state law says about going back to court. Here are some questions to ask yourself to help figure out what are your chances for claiming a pension share now.

Was the Pension Overlooked?

If the pension was not awarded to either you or your husband, or even mentioned at the time of your divorce, you may still have a chance to get a share. In a few states, such as California and Texas, recent court decisions and new state laws have allowed a former wife to ask for a share of an "overlooked" pension years after the divorce.

Even if you divorced in a state that usually does not divide overlooked pensions (such as Mississippi), you may be able to claim a pension share if you and your ex-husband ever lived together while married in a division-after-divorce state (such as California). You may be successful in going back to court in the no-division-after-divorce state if that state says it will use, in deciding your rights, the divorce law of the state where you were "domiciled" when the pension was earned. Such a rule might let you get a share of the pension earned while you and your husband were living in the division-after-divorce state.

IMPORTANT: If your ex-husband has died, you are probably out of luck as far as getting benefits goes, no matter what the reasons were that you weren't awarded a pension share at divorce. Once a retiree dies, there are usually no more pension benefits to be paid, unless *previous* arrangements had been made to pay a survivor. For you as an ex-wife, such an arrangement would usually mean that a court had awarded you a widow's pension or that, after your divorce, your ex-husband voluntarily named you to receive a widow's pension, assuming his retirement system allowed him to do so. Retirement systems rarely provide an *automatic* widow's pension to an ex-wife.

Was Your Ex-husband Awarded the Whole Pension?

It is most difficult to get a pension share awarded after divorce if the original divorce court awarded the entire pension to your ex-husband or if you signed a property settlement or separation agreement which provided the pension to your ex-husband. A new court will normally assume that you already had your chance to try to get part of the pension.

Were You Defrauded?

Occasionally, a former wife ends up without a pension share because, at the time of divorce, her husband concealed the fact that he had a pension, or deliberately misrepresented his benefits, or refused to provide important information about them. Unfortunately, once your divorce is final, a later court probably won't let you ask for a share based on his fraud, because courts usually say that it is the responsibility of each party in a divorce case to investigate and prove the facts before the case is first decided. You may be in a better position to challenge his concealment, however, if your property settlement contains a statement to the effect that husband and wife have each made a full disclosure of his or her assets.

Or a court may be more willing to give you another chance to claim those benefits if your ex-husband used serious threats or coercion to prevent you from taking advantage of your pension rights.

The laws on fraud in a divorce vary from state to state. If you believe there was a pension "cover-up," talk to a lawyer. State law may require you to make your claim within a short time — possibly within one year — after your divorce.

Are You Receiving Alimony?

Sometimes, even after the divorce, a court may agree that a divorced wife should be paid a pension share as alimony or support. *If you are already collecting alimony,* a court may be willing to increase your payment — and have the alimony paid from the pension — if you can show that there has been a "substantial change in circumstances." For example, if, compared to when you were divorced, you now need a greater amount of support, or your ex-husband has a greater ability to pay, you may be able to persuade the court to order that part of your ex-husband's pension should be used to increase your alimony.

The fact that your ex-husband has retired and started collecting his pension since your divorce is not, in itself, a reason for the court to give you an increase in alimony. In fact, a worker is likely to have a lower income after retirement, which might give your ex-husband a reason to ask the court to *reduce* your alimony.

Did Your Lawyer Commit Malpractice?

A few ex-wives have successfully sued their former divorce lawyers for malpractice because the lawyers did not protect their clients' pension rights. You may have grounds to sue your former lawyer *if* you can show that the lawyer's wrong advice or lack of advice was the reason you didn't get your pension share. Your lawyer has the duty to research the law that applies to your case, and to find out what assets your husband has and how much they are worth.

But the fact that your divorce lawyer did not ask for a pension share does not necessarily mean that there was malpractice if state divorce law or the retirement system rules *at the time of your divorce* didn't definitely provide for pension division. Many of the laws relating to pensions have only been developed in recent years.

If the court agrees that there was malpractice, your former lawyer may be required to pay you an amount of money equal to the pension share you would have been awarded at divorce if you had been properly represented.

If you think your divorce lawyer did not protect your rights, you may want to get the advice of a lawyer who specializes in legal malpractice to find out whether you have a case. Be sure to find out what legal time limits may apply to filing a malpractice case.

Will the New Pension Reforms Help You?

You may have heard about laws passed since your divorce giving new pension rights to former wives. The problem is that most of these reforms are not retroactive: that is, they do not right old wrongs. In general, the law that applies to your case is the law that was in effect at the time your divorce became final.

Although Congress has enacted many protections for divorced spouses in the last few years, there is still *no* federal law that *requires* pensions to be divided. The decision about whether to divide the pension remains with the state courts. But you should read the section in *Part Three* of this handbook concerning the particular type of retirement system involved in your case to see how changes in federal law might affect you.

If your ex-husband worked under a state or local government retirement system, you or your lawyer may want to contact that retirement system to find out whether there have been any changes in plan rules that would apply to already divorced spouses.

While a number of state divorce laws have improved and now say that pensions *must* be treated as a marital asset at divorce, most of these state law changes apply only to divorces that take place *after* the laws go into effect. Although there are rare exceptions, these new laws usually do not authorize a court to reconsider a final divorce decree or make a pension award after divorce.

Should You Take Action?

If you believe you did not get the pension benefits to which you were entitled, talk to a lawyer who specializes in family law to find out what the law says about your situation. This section has given only general guidelines about getting a pension share after divorce: the laws in this area can and do change, usually in favor of ex-wives.

If your lawyer says you might be successful in claiming a pension share now, then you will need to figure out whether going back to court would be worthwhile. If you would be asking for a share of a pension as marital property, keep in mind that, at best, you would probably be able to share in only that part of the pension earned during your marriage.

If you were divorced years ago and most of your ex-husband's work under his retirement system took place *after* your divorce, then it is likely that you could share in only a small part of his pension.

Also consider: If you do win your case, how will you *collect* your share? What can you do if your ex-husband refuses to pay you?

Compare the benefits you stand to gain against the necessary time and expense of pursuing legal action.

PART THREE

A GUIDE TO SPECIFIC RETIREMENT SYSTEMS:

WHAT ARE YOUR RIGHTS?

Part Three describes the largest retirement systems and explains how the rules of each affect pension rights at divorce. Each chapter tells you what benefits are available from a specific retirement system and how to claim them.

CHAPTER 1

SOCIAL SECURITY

SOCIAL SECURITY

How Social Security Works

The social security retirement system covers workers in private companies and nonprofit organizations, members of the military, and civilian employees of the federal government hired in 1984 and after.* It also covers about 70 percent of state and local government employees, some employees of religious organizations, and people who are self-employed. It is run by the Social Security Administration, a federal agency.

Both employers and employees are required to pay into social security. A worker born after 1928 needs to have at least 10 years of work under social security in order to earn benefits at retirement. Fewer years of work are needed for workers born before 1929. The monthly benefit a worker receives is based on the number of years worked and the worker's average earnings, but not on how much money was paid in.

A worker born before 1938 may start collecting a basic social security retirement benefit at age 65, or a reduced benefit as early as age 62. (The retirement age for a worker born in 1938 or later depends on the worker's year of birth and ranges up to age 67.)

A worker who qualifies for social security disability may start collecting the unreduced basic social security benefit at any age.

Everyone who receives social security benefits, including family members, gets yearly cost of living increases.

---

* Federal government employees hired before 1984 were given the chance to transfer to a new retirement system that included social security coverage for future years of work.

Social Security Benefits for Divorced Wives

You may be eligible for social security benefits based on your ex-husband's work if you meet certain requirements and make an application for benefits through a social security office. (*See* "Getting Information," page 64.) No court order is necessary. Benefits can be paid both while your ex-husband is living and after he dies. (Note that the Social Security Administration uses the word "wife" to refer to a woman whose husband is living, and "widow" or "mother" to refer to someone whose husband has died or to a widow with children.)

IMPORTANT: If you are counting on receiving both pension benefits and a large social security benefit from your husband's work, you need to know that social security "offsets" can cancel out some or all of the social security benefits you may expect to receive. (*See* "Offsets," page 58.) Don't give up the right to other property or financial settlements at divorce until you know whether your social security benefits may be affected.

Your Rights While Your Ex-husband Is Living

A former wife who was married at least 10 years may be eligible for a social security benefit based on her ex-husband's earnings even if his social security credits were not earned during the marriage. This divorced wife benefit is not taken out of the ex-husband's social security check, but is a separate benefit equal to no more than half of his basic benefit. (It is the same amount as a wife's benefit.) You may start collecting the benefit as early as age 62, but it will be reduced — up to 25 percent — if you start collecting before age 65.* For example, if you could collect *$200* a month starting at 65, you could instead choose to collect *$150* a month starting at 62.

* If you were born after 1937, the maximum reduction may be as much as 35 percent, depending on the year you were born.

In order to receive a divorced wife benefit:

- You must be at least 62 years old, *and*
- You must not have remarried since your divorce, *and*
- The marriage must have lasted at least 10 years, *and*
- Your former husband must have begun collecting his own retirement or disability benefits,

    OR

    If he is not yet collecting, he must be at least age 62 and have worked long enough to earn the right to receive social security retirement benefits, and you must have been divorced at least two years.

The divorced wife benefit can be paid for as long as your ex-husband lives, although certain events can cause your benefits to stop sooner. (*See* "Factors That Can Affect Your Benefits," page 55.)

Social security does not pay a disability benefit to a divorced wife who is or becomes disabled (but does pay a benefit to a divorced disabled *widow*).

Note: Courts occasionally consider the *ex-husband's* social security benefit as part of the marital property or as a resource on which to base an award of alimony or child support. A court might do this even if you were not married 10 years.

Your Rights After Your Ex-husband Dies

After your ex-husband dies, you may be eligible for one of three survivor benefits.

- A *divorced widow benefit* is payable if you were married at least 10 years and are at least age 60.

- A *disabled divorced widow benefit* is payable if you were married at least 10 years and are at least age 50 and severely disabled.

- A *surviving divorced mother benefit* is payable regardless of the length of your marriage or how young you are, as long as you have in your care the worker's child who is under age 16 or disabled and is collecting a social security benefit.

The first two benefits, the divorced widow and disabled divorced widow benefits, are equal to 100 percent of the benefit your former husband was collecting (or would have collected, if he dies before retirement). Your benefit will be reduced if you start collecting it before age 65. For example, a maximum reduction of 28 1/2 percent applies if you start collecting at age 60 or earlier.

A surviving divorced mother benefit is equal to 75 percent of your ex-husband's age-65 benefit. Your age does not affect the amount you receive.

Don't Delay In Applying

Even if you have lost track of your ex-husband and don't know whether he has retired or died (or you don't know his social security number), you should apply for benefits if you think you might be eligible. The Social Security Administration can help you obtain the necessary information.

Factors That Can Affect Your Benefits

You may lose all or part of your expected benefits if you remarry, work after retirement, or collect more than one benefit.

Remarriage

If you remarry, your divorced spouse benefits may well be affected.

- *Divorced Wife*. This benefit stops if you remarry at any age. It can be restored, however, if your new marriage ends.

- *Surviving Divorced Mother*. This benefit stops if you remarry at any age, but can be restored if your new marriage ends and you still have an eligible child in your care. But even if this benefit stops, you may eventually become eligible for a divorced widow benefit once you meet the age and other requirements.

- *Divorced Widow*. You cannot collect this benefit if you remarry before age 60, unless your new marriage ends through the death of your new husband, divorce, or annulment.

- *Disabled Divorced Widow*. If you remarry before you are age 50 and become disabled, you cannot collect this benefit. However, you can become eligible for benefits if your new marriage ends through the death of your new husband, divorce, or annulment.

If your ex-husband remarries, your divorced spouse social security benefits will not be affected. (The fact that his wife or another ex-wife collects a spouse benefit does not affect your benefit.)

Note: If you are eligible to collect two social security spouse benefits because you were married twice, you can receive an amount equal to the larger of the two benefits, but not both.

Work After Retirement: The "Earnings Test"

Whether you receive a social security benefit as a worker or spouse, the social security *earnings test* applies to you if you are under age 70. The earnings test means that if you have earnings over a certain amount within a calendar year, you can lose part or all of your social security benefits for that year. The exact amount you can earn before you start losing social security benefits increases each year, and varies according to your age. Disabled workers and spouses have additional restrictions on earnings.

The ex-husband's work after retirement will not reduce his divorced wife's benefit.

For more information on how work after retirement can affect your benefits, contact a social security office.

"Offsets" of Benefits From Other Work

If you have worked and earned your own social security benefit, or you *or* your ex-husband earned a state, local, or federal government pension, these benefits may offset, or cancel out, your divorced spouse benefit. You may end up receiving less in social security divorced spouse benefits than you had expected.

How Your Own Social Security May Affect Your Benefits as a Divorced Wife or Widow: The Dual Entitlement Rule

If you are entitled to a social security benefit through your own work in addition to a social security benefit as a divorced spouse, the Social Security Administration will deduct an amount equal to *your* worker benefit, dollar for dollar, from your benefit as a divorced spouse. The result is that you will be paid only an amount equal to the larger of the two benefits, but not the sum of the two. The Social Security Administration calls this "dual entitlement."

■ Example 1

Irene's social security worker benefit is $300. As a divorced wife, she would be eligible for a divorced wife benefit of $210 (50 percent of her ex-husband's benefit of $420). But since $300 (her own worker benefit) is more than $210 (the divorced wife benefit), she will receive only her $300 a month benefit as a retired worker, not $510 (the sum of the two benefits).

	After Offset	If No Offset
Social Security worker benefit	$300	$300
Social Security spouse benefit	$0	$210
TOTAL	$300	$510

■ Example 2

Through her own job, Helen has earned a social security worker benefit of $180. As a divorced wife, she would be eligible for a spouse benefit of $250 a month (50 percent of her ex-husband's benefit of $500). But her own worker benefit of $180 will be deducted from $250, leaving her only $70 to be paid as a divorced wife. She will still get her own $180 worker benefit plus $70 as her divorced wife benefit. She will end up getting $250, not $430.

	After Offset	If No Offset
Social Security spouse benefit	$70	$250
Social Security worker benefit	$180	$180
TOTAL	$250	$430

How your Own Government Pension May Affect Your Benefits as a Divorced Wife or Widow: The Government Pension Offset Rule

If you earned or will earn a pension by working as a federal, state, or local government employee, and you were not also covered by social security on the same job as of the last day of your employment, part of your government pension may be deducted from your social security divorced spouse benefit. This is the "Government Pension Offset" Rule.

If the offset applies to you, then an amount equal to two-thirds of your government pension will be subtracted from your social security divorced spouse benefit. If two-thirds of your government pension is more than your social security spouse benefit, you won't be able to collect any part of that social security benefit. (The Government Pension Offset Rule does not affect the amount of your government pension, only your social security benefit.)

If your ex-husband were to be awarded part of your government pension in the divorce, then two-thirds of only the *remaining* portion of your government pension would be offset from your social security spouse benefit.

■ Examples

Eileen was first eligible in 1985 for her government pension of $600 a month, which she earned as a public school teacher. As a divorced widow, she also would have been eligible for a $500 a month benefit from social security (based on the amount her ex-husband had collected). But she will actually receive a social security divorced widow benefit of $500 *minus* two-thirds of $600.

Here is the way her benefit will be figured:

$$\text{Social Security spouse benefit} \quad - \quad \frac{2}{3}\left\{\text{Government pension}\right\} = \text{Social Security spouse benefit payable}$$

$$\$500 \quad - \quad \frac{2}{3}\,(\$600) = \text{Social Security spouse benefit payable}$$

$$\$500 \quad - \quad \$400 \quad = \quad \$100$$

	After Offset	If No Offset
Government pension	$600	$600
Social Security spouse benefit	$100	$500
TOTAL	$700	$1100

Eileen will collect her $600 government pension and $100 from social security.

- -

Vera's federal government pension is $900 a month. As a divorced wife, she would have been eligible for $350 a month from social security (50 percent of her ex-husband's benefit of $700 a month). Two-thirds of $900 (her government pension) is $600. Since $600 is more than her $350-a-month social security benefit, she will receive no benefit from social security.

	After Offset	If No Offset
Government pension	$900	$900
Social Security spouse benefit	$0	$350
TOTAL	$900	$1250

Exceptions to Government Pension Offset Rule

The offset does not apply to you if you meet any one of the following three exceptions:

- You filed for a social security spouse benefit before December 1977.

- You became eligible to receive your government pension before December 1982 and you were married at least 20 years. (Being "eligible" does not necessarily mean you were actually collecting your government pension.)

- You were eligible to receive your government pension before July 1983 and you were receiving at least one-half of your financial support from your husband or ex-husband just before he retired, died (before retirement), or became disabled.

These exceptions are the result of changes in the social security law which were made in 1977, 1982, and 1983.

More Reductions: The "Windfall Penalty Rule"

If your ex-husband earned a social security worker benefit from one job and a government pension from a different job that was not covered by social security, his social security worker benefit could be reduced. This, in turn, could reduce your social security divorced spouse benefit, because your benefit is based on the amount he receives. The reduction is called the "Windfall Penalty Rule" and applies if:

- Your ex-husband did not work under social security for at least 30 years, *and*

- He was not *eligible* to collect his social security benefit or government pension before 1986. (Being "eligible" does not necessarily mean he was actually collecting benefits.)

The Windfall Penalty Rule uses a complicated formula to recalculate and reduce a worker's social security benefit.

How much the worker's social security benefit is reduced varies from person to person. This formula takes into account the year in which the worker was born, his average earnings, the number of years he worked under social security, and other facts.

The Windfall Penalty Rule can reduce a social security worker benefit by as much as 55 percent, but the reduction in social security can never be an amount greater than half the government pension.

This rule only reduces social security benefits while the worker is receiving his government pension. If your ex-husband dies first, you will be able to receive a social security divorced widow benefit in full, along with any government widow's pension to which you may be entitled.

IMPORTANT: If *you* worked and earned your own social security benefit from one job, but also earned your own government pension from another job that was not covered by social security, *your* social security benefit may be reduced by the Windfall Penalty Rule.

Contact the Social Security Administration to find out how this rule might affect your benefit.

■ Example 1

Here is how the Windfall Penalty Rule might apply in a "worst case":

Vernon, who was born in 1929, earned a monthly social security benefit of $287 after working 10 years under social security. He also has a federal government pension of $950 a month from his work as a letter carrier with the U.S. Postal Service. As a result of the Windfall Penalty Rule, he loses 55 percent of his social security benefit and ends up collecting only $130 a month in addition to his government pension. Therefore, his ex-wife Bernice receives a social security divorced wife benefit equal to 50 percent of $130, or $65 a month.

A Triple Reduction

If either you or your ex-husband worked under a government retirement system, and at least one of you worked under social security, there is a good chance that you will be affected by more than one "offset."

Note: In a situation where more than one offset may apply, it is usually easier to first figure out how much the social security *worker* benefit(s) will be.

Here's an example involving all three types of reductions.

■ Example

Evelyn worked off and on as a secretary in small offices in the early years of her marriage. Through this work, she accumulated a social security benefit of $400 a month. Once divorce seemed imminent, she got a regular clerical job with the federal government, and earned a small civil service pension of $240 a month.

Her now ex-husband Ed spent his entire career in private industry and recently retired from his job as a credit manager with a social security benefit of $720. Evelyn's divorced spouse benefit would be equal to 50 percent of $720, or $360.

If Evelyn could receive all her benefits in full, her monthly retirement income would be:

Government pension	$240
Social Security worker benefit	$400
Social Security divorced spouse benefit	$360
TOTAL	$1000

But see what happens to her benefits:

1. *Windfall Penalty Rule.* This reduction involves her government pension and her social security worker benefit.

    Government pension $240

    Social Security worker benefit $400 ⇨ reduced to $280

    In Evelyn's particular case, the Windfall Penalty Rule left her with a social security worker benefit of $280.

    Next, see how much the social security spouse benefit will be. First, see if it will be reduced by the *Dual Entitlement Rule.* Then, apply the *Government Pension Offset Rule.* In this case, we start out with Evelyn's basic divorced wife benefit of $360 (50 percent of $720, Ed's worker benefit).

2. *Dual Entitlement Rule.* This reduction counts her social security worker benefit, or the remaining portion of it — $280 — against her social security spouse benefit of $360: $360 minus $280 is $80 .

    Social Security worker benefit $280

    Social Security spouse benefit $360 ⇨ reduced to $80

3. *Government Pension Offset Rule.* This reduction involves her government pension and her social security spouse benefit (which is now down to $80). The government pension is $240. Two-thirds of $240 is $160. Since $160 is more than her $80 social security spouse benefit, the social security benefit is completely offset and she collects nothing as a spouse.

    Government pension $240

    Social Security spouse benefit $ 80 ⇨ reduced to $0

Here's what Evelyn ends up with:

	After Offset	If No Offset
Government pension	$240	$240
Social Security worker benefit	$280	$400
Social Security spouse benefit	$0	$360
TOTAL	$520	$1000

Instead of $1000 a month, she receives $520 a month.

Getting Information

By calling the Social Security Administration's toll-free telephone number (800) 772-1213, you can request general information, social security publications, and an estimate of your social security benefits. Calls are answered between 7:00 a.m. and 7:00 p.m. weekdays. You can also receive free assistance through your local social security office. See your telephone "white pages" for office locations.

CHAPTER 2

PRIVATE PENSIONS

IMPORTANT: The federal law on pensions described in this chapter does not apply to some retirement plans run by religious organizations or international organizations, such as the World Bank or the United Nations. It also does not apply to certain plans for highly-paid company executives over and above the regular company pension plan. If your husband earned benefits under one of these plans, you might have difficulty collecting your share, even if the benefits are marital property. Your lawyer should check with the plan to see whether it will honor any domestic relations orders. If not, you may have to collect your share from your ex-husband, rather than the plan, or trade your share for another marital asset of equal value.

PRIVATE PENSIONS

How Private Pensions Work

Approximately one-half of all employees working for private companies are covered by a private retirement plan, typically, an employee pension plan set up by a company, or set up by an agreement between a union and one or more companies. Employees are usually not required to pay into private plans. There are different types of pension plans, and an employee may be included in more than one kind of plan on the same job. Also, a company may have separate plans for different groups of employees, such as hourly and salaried employees, or union and non-union employees.

In addition to having pension plans, employees may be covered by other kinds of private retirement plans such as profit-sharing plans, deferred compensation plans, thrift and "401(k)" savings plans, and employee stock ownership plans (ESOPs).

Benefits from any of these plans may be considered marital assets at divorce.

Although the provisions of private plans vary a great deal, all these plans must meet minimum standards established by federal laws. These laws include the Employee Retirement Income Security Act of 1974 (ERISA) and the Internal Revenue Code.

This chapter discusses the pension rights that every company and union plan is required by law to provide for spouses at divorce. Because plans are so different, specific company plans are not described here.

Rights to Benefits

Private pension plans typically require that employees must work a specified number of years to earn the right to receive a pension at retirement age. The number of years required to earn the right to a pension under a plan ranges from one to ten years. When an employee has earned this right he is said to be *"vested."*

Calculating Benefits

Pension plans use different formulas to figure benefits. In many plans, benefits are based on a percentage of pay multiplied by the number of years of work under the plan. A plan may be either of two types: a plan that pays out a specific benefit at retirement *("defined benefit")* or one that specifies how much the employer pays into the plan *("defined contribution")*. (*See* "How Do Pension Plans Work?" page 10.)

Very few private pension plans increase benefits for inflation automatically each year. Some plans provide occasional cost of living adjustments.

Retirement Age

An employee who is vested is eligible to collect a pension at least by age 65. But most plans allow employees to retire earlier, for example, by age 55 or 60, usually with reduced benefits.

Forms of Payment

The basic form of payment for a single retiree is a life annuity, that is, a monthly pension paid for the retiree's life. For a married retiree, the basic form is a *"joint and survivor"* annuity. This is a reduced pension that, upon the employee's death, will pay a surviving spouse a lifetime pension of 50 percent of the reduced amount. (*See* "Words to Know," page 77.)

Some plans may let the retiree choose a *"lump sum"* (one-time) payment, but plans are not required to offer lump sums. For certain types of retirement plans, however, such as profit-sharing plans, the basic form of payment *is* the lump sum.

Disability Pensions

Disability pensions, if they are offered, are often payable earlier than regular pensions. A company is not required to provide disability pensions.

Plan Administration and Regulation

Each plan is run by its own "plan administrator," the person responsible for the day-to-day operation of the plan.

Private pension law is regulated and enforced by three federal agencies: the U.S. Department of Labor, the Internal Revenue Service, and the Pension Benefit Guaranty Corporation.

Private Pension Benefits for Divorced Wives

A court may award you a share of your former husband's private pension at divorce and allow you to begin collecting your benefit while he is still working, after he retires, or after he dies.

State laws guide the court's decisions about how much you will get, and about whether the pension is to be divided as marital property or used as a source of alimony or support. (Or, the couple may decide these issues as part of their property settlement.)

The court may decide whether the payments will be paid by your former husband or by the pension plan. If the court (or property settlement) provides for the pension plan to make payments directly to you, *the court award must be in a specific form, called a "Qualified Domestic Relations*

Order" or *QDRO*. In this chapter, the QDRO is often called a "court order," even though it is really a special type of court order. To find out the rules for awarding you a pension share through a QDRO, the court follows federal law. The rights of a divorced spouse under a QDRO were created by the Retirement Equity Act of 1984. This Act amended ERISA, the federal law on private pensions, and went into effect in 1985.

What Is a Qualified Domestic Relations Order?

A "qualified domestic relations order" (QDRO) is a state court order, judgment, or decree, or a court-approved property settlement agreement, that says a private pension plan is to pay a share of an employee's or retiree's pension to an "alternate payee" (that is, someone else). The alternate payee can be a spouse, former spouse, child, or other dependent. *The major difference between a qualified domestic relations order and the order (or property settlement) you would normally get as part of your divorce is that the QDRO contains certain detailed information about the pension and is sent to the plan (usually by the former wife).*

Your Rights While Your Ex-husband Is Living

Private pension plans, unlike social security, do not have separate benefits for the divorced wife of a living employee or retiree. However, a court may award you a share of the worker's pension when you divorce.

In general, the choices you have about when you can start collecting benefits and how much you can collect depend on the options your former husband has under his pension plan. But there are some special rules that apply to payments made through a QDRO.

How Soon Can You Collect?

The law on private pensions permits an ex-wife to start collecting her pension share before her husband retires. However, federal pension law (and often state divorce law) places some limits on early payments.

One restriction under pension law is that the plan doesn't have to pay you before your ex-husband has met certain requirements for getting a pension himself. For example, your share can be paid out only after the employee becomes *"vested"* under the rules of the plan. That is, he must have been employed for the number of years needed to earn the right to a benefit under the plan. Also, you can't begin collecting until your ex-husband reaches a certain age or meets other requirements for paying benefits to employees.

The court order may require the plan to make payments to you only after:

- Your former husband has stopped working under the plan, and is eligible to start collecting his pension (even if he hasn't yet applied for it),

Or, if you want to collect while he's still working,

- He has reached the earliest age for collecting benefits under the plan (early retirement) and is at least age 50,

OR,

He has reached the earliest date that he could collect without having to leave the job. (Only a few plans have provisions to pay an employee while he's still working.)

■ Example

Donald, age 47, works for a small hardware company that has a profit-sharing plan. He has worked long enough to become vested. His plan provides that he can receive his benefits, which will be paid in a lump sum, whenever he terminates his employment (that is, leaves his job), but the plan will not pay him any benefits while he is still on the job. Donald says he expects to keep working as long as he can.

He and his wife Nancy are in the process of divorcing and have agreed that she will receive a lump sum of $15,000 from his plan. Nancy wants to be paid as soon as possible after the divorce. Under the rules described above, the law would permit the plan to pay Nancy her share when Donald leaves his job, no matter what his age. But if she wants her share while he's still working, she'll have to wait until he reaches age 50.

Their QDRO can be written to provide that the plan will pay her $15,000 of Donald's benefits as soon as he reaches age 50 or stops working, whichever comes first.

Even if your divorce occurs before benefits become payable, you can get a court order that provides for payments to start at the time the law allows the benefits to be paid out.

Check for Special Provisions

The law allows a plan to have special provisions for early payment under a QDRO. This would mean that an ex-wife could be paid even before the employee reaches the plan's official retirement age (the age at which an employee can be paid). It is unusual for a plan to have such a provision, but if you want to be paid your share as soon as possible, your lawyer may want to find out whether your husband's plan has a special provision for early payment under a QDRO.

Reasons to Wait

Although the law permits you to withdraw your pension share while your former husband is still working under the plan, you might not want to do this if his plan gives more pension benefits for work done toward the end of an employee's career.

Some plans increase benefits dramatically as an employee gets closer to age 65. Other plans pay special large early retirement pensions to people who complete 20 years or 30 years of employment and work up to a certain age. If your ex-husband's plan offers such benefits, the amount of his pension might, for example, suddenly double or triple in his twentieth year under the plan.

You also may want to wait to collect your share if your ex-husband's plan includes a special "social security supplement" or "bridge benefit" that is added to early retirement benefits until a retired worker reaches age 62. A social security supplement is usually an amount equal to what a worker's social security benefit will be at age 62. (A retired worker cannot get social security retirement benefits before age 62.) The reason for waiting is that the law says that your share cannot include part of your ex-husband's social security supplement while he is still working under the plan. Your QDRO can be written so that you will get a share of the supplement once your husband leaves his job.

If you want to start collecting your share right away *and* also share in the larger benefits that your ex-husband may earn later, your QDRO will have to be specifically written to increase your share as your ex-husband's benefits increase. But you may find it difficult to persuade your husband or the court to agree to this kind of early payment arrangement.

You should also be aware that a plan administrator may attempt to discourage you from asking for earlier payments since making early payments can be more trouble, and in some cases more costly, for the plan. Occasionally, plan officials will try to bill the divorcing wife for some of these costs. The law does not say whether this practice is legal or not.

Monthly Pension or Lump Sum?

A QDRO (Qualified Domestic Relations Order) can require a plan to pay you your share of the pension in any form of payment that the plan offers to your husband. For example, if the plan offers employees a choice of a lifetime monthly pension or a lump sum, the order might specify which form you are to receive, but it could just say that you will have the right to select one of the options available when your share of the pension becomes payable.

   If your court order specifically provides for it, you could be paid your share in the form of a pension over *your life*. Your share of your ex-husband's pension will be refigured according to how long a person of your age can be expected to live. Getting your share as a pension for your life, or as a "life annuity," means that your benefit will be paid as long as you live, even if you outlive your ex-husband. Having your share paid in this form is one way of making sure your benefits continue after your ex-husband dies. (Another way to be sure of getting benefits after his death is by including a provision for a widow's pension in your court order. *See* page 75.)

Your Choices May Be Limited

If your divorce occurs after your husband has started collecting his pension, the plan can say that the form of benefit he is collecting cannot be changed. What this means is that your share of his pension has to be paid out of the benefits in the form he has already selected for himself.

   Plans may *require* that you be paid benefits in the form of a lump sum if the total value of your share is $3500 or less.

Minimizing Your Taxes

In general, you can expect to pay taxes on your pension share. If you receive your share in a lump sum, you may be able to avoid paying taxes all at once by transferring all or part of the lump sum to an Individual Retirement Account within 60 days after you receive your share. You won't have to pay taxes on the funds deposited into the IRA until you withdraw the money later. (*See* Chapter 3, "Individual Retirement Accounts.") Even if you don't put the lump sum into an IRA, you still may be able to reduce your taxes by using special "averaging" rules that apply to pension lump sums. Ask your lawyer or the Internal Revenue Service for more information about these rules.

How Much Can You Get?

Federal law doesn't specify any particular amount that a former wife can be awarded — it just says that you can't be awarded any more than 100 percent of your husband's pension. The court will be guided by state law to help it decide the size of your share. (*See* Part Two, "State Divorce Law and Your Pension Rights," page 17.)

If your court order does not specify the amount you are to be paid in dollars, then you need to make sure that the order spells out how your share is to be figured. For example, the court order could specify that you are to be paid a certain fraction or percentage of the pension.

For details on sending your court order to the plan, see "Understanding Your Court Order (QDRO)," page 85.

Your Rights After Your Ex-husband Dies

Once you are divorced, you will probably lose whatever widow's pension protection you may have had while married unless your QDRO specifically provides for a widow's pension. (*But see* Box on next page.)

One way for the QDRO to provide a widow's pension is for the order to say that the former wife is to be treated as a surviving spouse. This would mean that you would receive the same widow's pension that you would have received had you remained married (typically, an amount equal to 50 percent of the benefit your husband was receiving). On the other hand, if you and your husband were married for only a portion of his career under his pension plan, a court might award you only a portion of the widow's pension. If your ex-husband remarried, his next wife would probably be eligible for the rest of the widow's pension. A widow's pension may also be shared by two or more former spouses.

A widow's benefit is payable only if the worker is vested in his pension at the time of his death.

If You Don't Have a Court Order

Even without a QDRO, you may have two possible ways to collect:

Divorce After Retirement. If you were divorced after your ex-husband started collecting his pension, you may be eligible to receive a widow's pension *if*:

- Your former husband retired in 1985 or after, *and*

- He took a reduced pension to give you a widow's pension (a Qualified Joint and Survivor Annuity-*see* next page).

Divorce Before Retirement. If you were divorced and your ex-husband died before he got a pension, you may be eligible to receive a widow's pension if:

- Both his work under the plan and your divorce were in 1985 or after (when a new law on widows' pensions went into effect),

- Your former husband did not remarry, *and*

- He did not exercise the plan's option to waive the survivor pension either during your marriage (which would have required your written consent) or after the divorce.

If your former husband has died, you should write his company's pension plan administrator to see whether you are entitled to a survivor annuity. If the plan administrator turns down your request but you think the decision may be wrong, you should see a lawyer.

When Can You Collect?

Your widow's pension cannot start any earlier than it would have if you had still been married to your husband at the time of his death.

If he dies before the plan's early retirement age for employees, you can usually choose to have your widow's pension start as early as the year that he would have reached that age. Even if your former husband dies before early retirement age, your widow's pension may be paid immediately if his plan was a "defined contribution" plan, such as a profit sharing plan. (*See* page 10.)

If he had already reached early retirement age or had started collecting his pension by the time of his death, your benefit can start immediately.

Words to Know

The name for a widow's pension varies from plan to plan, but federal law has official names for the two types of widows' benefits that every pension plan must provide. A divorced wife may be entitled to these benefits if her court order says she is to be treated as a surviving spouse, or specifically provides these benefits.

A *Qualified Joint and Survivor Annuity* (QJSA) is the name of the benefit a married employee receives at retirement. It is a husband-and-wife pension, that is, a benefit reduced for the employee so as to leave something for the surviving spouse. It is called a "joint" annuity (or pension) because it can be paid over two lifetimes — first to the retired worker, then to the surviving spouse. Under federal law, the widow's pension must usually be equal to at least 50 percent of the reduced pension the retiree was collecting. The exact reduction in the retiree's pension varies from plan to plan.

The plan is likely to provide that if the wife dies first, the retiree will continue receiving his reduced pension even though no widow's pension will be payable.

■ Example 1

Alfred's pension at retirement is $200 a month, if payable as a pension for his life only. But since he is married, the benefit will be paid as a husband-and-wife pension (QJSA) and he receives $180 a month for his lifetime. If he dies first, his wife Iris will get 50 percent of that amount, or $90 a month, for her lifetime. If she dies first, he will continue to receive $180 a month.

A number of plans also offer in addition to the 50 percent widow's pension, larger widows' pensions, such as 75 or 100 percent, usually requiring a greater reduction in the retiree's pension.

A Qualified Pre-retirement Survivor Annuity (QPSA) is the name of the benefit a widow receives if her husband dies before he starts collecting his pension. Once you are divorced, you can collect this benefit if your court order specifies that you receive it. Your benefit would be equal to 50 percent of the amount your ex-husband would have received, based on his work up to the date of death. You can start receiving your benefit at least by the year that he would have reached the earliest retirement age under the plan, or at age 55, whichever is later. If he had already reached retirement age, your benefit will start immediately after his death.

■ Example 2

Richard died at age 51 in 1994, while still working under his company pension plan. If he had lived, he would have been eligible for a pension of $600 a month starting at age 55, in 1998. His ex-wife Faith will therefore be entitled to a widow's pension of $300 a month (50 percent of $600) starting in 1998.

The Pre-retirement Survivor Annuity and the Joint and Survivor Annuity are considered separate benefits. For example, even if you gave up your right to the Pre-retirement Survivor Annuity while you were married, you may still be entitled to the Joint and Survivor Annuity unless you specifically gave up that benefit, too.

If You Die First

Federal law does not say what happens to your share of the pension if you die first. If your QDRO says your share is to be paid as an annuity over your lifetime and payments had begun, the benefits would probably stop at your death and not go back to your ex-husband. But if you are to get your benefits "if, as and when" the pension is paid to your former husband, then your share will probably go back to him when you die. In some states, the divorce court might order the pension plan to pay your remaining share of the pension to your heirs, but you cannot "will" your benefits to someone else.

If your former husband had been receiving a reduced pension to pay for your widow's pension, the plan may say that he must continue receiving the reduction, but that the widow's pension will not be paid to anyone else. Some plans will allow a retiree in this situation to resume receiving his full pension, or to designate his new wife to receive the widow's pension.

Your Written Consent Needed to Sign Away Survivor Annuity

A married employee ordinarily must get his wife's written consent in order to receive pension benefits in any form other than the reduced monthly pension that would provide a widow's pension after his death (a QJSA). He must also get his wife's consent if he does not want a widow's pension paid if he dies before he retires (a QPSA).

For example, while you are still married, your husband must get your consent in order to provide a survivor's pension for someone else (such as a child), to take an unreduced pension for his life only, to take a lump sum, or to borrow against his benefits. (Some plans, such as profit sharing plans, may allow a worker to borrow against as much as 50 percent of his vested benefits.)

Your consent to give up a widow's pension must be in writing, and be witnessed by a plan official or a notary public. The law requires that the waiver form that you sign explain in understandable language that you are agreeing to give up a lifetime widow's pension. Unfortunately, however, most waiver forms are written in complicated legal language. Be careful what you sign - ask questions before signing any paper you don't fully understand.

Exceptions:
There are occasions when a wife's consent to give up a widow's pension is not required. These include:

- *The employee or retiree is not legally married.* But a divorced wife's consent *is* required if a Qualified Domestic Relations Order requires her consent or provides pension benefits to her.

- *The employee or retiree is* legally *separated or has been abandoned by his wife and has a court order indicating the separation or abandonment.* The fact that a couple has been living apart for many years does not, in itself, mean that the wife's consent is not required.

- *The employee or retiree can prove to the plan administrator that the wife cannot be located.*

- *The employee's plan is a type of plan not required to follow the usual consent rules.* Profit-sharing and other plans that normally pay benefits only in the form of a lump sum may specifically provide that, upon the worker's death, 100 percent of the funds in an employee's account is automatically paid to the surviving spouse, unless she has consented in writing to give up her rights.

If your husband's plan falls under the last exception, you will be protected *if* he dies while you are still married and the money is still in the plan, but he does not have to get your consent to withdraw or borrow against his benefits. The danger is that he will probably be able to withdraw all his benefits as soon as he leaves the job.

If your husband has benefits in one of these "exempt" plans, *you may need a QDRO or a preliminary court order to stop your husband from withdrawing the pension benefits without your consent even before you are divorced.*

Note: These consent requirements apply to your husband's pension if he was on the job or applied for his pension in 1985 or later. If he started collecting before 1985, the law did not require him to get your consent to give up the widow's pension.

If the Benefits Have Been Withdrawn

If you are going through a divorce and discover that your husband has already withdrawn benefits without your consent, there are circumstances in which the plan might still be required to pay you benefits under a QDRO as if your share had not been taken out of the pension plan. This situation could occur if, for example, your husband tells plan officials he is not married, or falsely claims not to know where you live, or forges your signature on a waiver form; or if plan officials simply neglect to ask him for your written consent. If a QDRO requires the plan to pay you a share of benefits that turn out to have been illegally withdrawn, the plan is likely to require your husband to give back to the plan the benefits he took out. But whether or not the plan ever succeeds in getting back the benefits from him does not affect your rights. The plan must still go ahead and pay you the benefits as required in your court order.

Factors That Can Affect Your Benefits

Certain events can reduce or eliminate your benefits. These can include remarriage, your ex-husband's return to work, or the termination of the plan.

Remarriage

Your ex-husband's new marriage or your own new marriage may affect your right to benefits *only if* your court order specifically says that remarriage will cause your benefits to stop.

Your Ex-husband Goes Back to Work

In some cases, pension plans are legally permitted to stop a retiree's benefits temporarily if he goes back to work. If your ex-husband's pension stops being paid, your share might also be stopped.

These rules are most likely to apply to your ex-husband if he is under age 65 and collecting a pension from a "multiemployer" plan, a plan where more than one company pays in under a union contract. Truck drivers and construction workers are examples of workers typically covered by this type of plan. The plan may say that if the retiree takes another job in the same "industry," even for a short time, all his benefits will be stopped (suspended) until he reaches age 65.

The law does not say what happens to the former wife's share if the retiree's benefits are stopped. What happens in your case might depend on the wording of your court order. The plan may try to stop your pension share if your court order specifically says that you are to be paid only as benefits are paid to your former husband. Your best argument for persuading the plan to continue payment is that the law does allow an ex-wife to collect benefits even if the retiree is not collecting. (*See* page 71.) Therefore, *your* pension share shouldn't be affected if his pension is temporarily stopped.

A plan's "suspension" of the retiree's pension does not affect your eligibility for a widow's pension.

The Plan Stops

A company can close down a pension plan if the plan is in serious financial trouble and if the company shows that it cannot afford to continue the plan. A plan can also be stopped for other reasons, but only if all the plan's benefits can be paid. When a plan is stopped, this is called a "plan termination." In a few situations, a plan termination can mean you will lose part or all of your pension share.

If a Plan Stops Because It Is in Financial Trouble

If a plan stops because it is in financial trouble, the worker's pension and your share of it may be protected by the government's pension insurance program run by the Pension Benefit Guaranty Corporation (PBGC), a federal agency. The pension, or most of it, is likely to be insured if it is from a *defined benefit* plan, that is, one with fixed benefit payouts.

Some Plans Not Insured

The PBGC does not insure defined benefit plans of professional firms with 25 or fewer employees, plans paid for by union dues only, plans run by religious organizations, or certain plans for company executives. The PBGC also does not insure *defined contribution* plans (plans that only specify what is paid in).

Some Benefits Not Insured

Although a plan may be insured by the PBGC, the insurance protection may not cover all benefits offered by the plan. Some benefits that may not be insured are:

- *Benefits Above Certain Levels.* For example, if a plan terminates in 1995, the maximum age-65 benefit insured is $2573.86 monthly. That is, any benefit over $2573.86 is not insured.

- *Benefits in a New Plan.* If a plan was started within five years before the plan stops, all or part of the benefits might not be insured.

- *New or Recently Improved Plan Benefits.* If certain plan benefits have been added or increased within five years before the plan stops, all or part of the new benefits might not be insured.

- *"Bridge" Benefits.* The PBGC usually does not insure special supplemental benefits (also known as "social security supplements") that are sometimes paid until a retiree reaches age 62 and becomes eligible for social security.

- *Disability Pension Benefits.* These benefits are not insured unless the benefits are being paid at the time the plan stops.

If your former husband's plan is insured, the PBGC will take over the plan's operation, and if the plan had already approved your court order, the PBGC will continue paying your share of the pension, or as much of it as is insured. If your court order is issued *after* the plan is taken over by the PBGC, then you should send your court order directly to the PBGC at:

Pension Benefit Guaranty Corporation
1200 K Street, NW
Washington, DC 20005
(202) 326-4000

Note: Call the PBGC first to speak to the person handling the particular pension plan, so that you can ask to whom to send the QDRO. When you call, it helps to know the date on which the plan terminated.

The PBGC has not yet issued regulations or written procedures about how it will handle QDROs. For now, you should expect that it will follow the same procedures the law requires for plans still in operation.

If a Plan Stops for Other Reasons

If a plan stops for a reason other than financial trouble, you should be able to receive all the benefits your QDRO provides. The company will transfer the plan money to an insurance company that will pay out benefits as the plan provided. If the plan had already accepted your court order before the plan termination, you can expect the insurance company to pay you in the same way as the QDRO required the plan to pay you. If your court order is issued after the termination, you will need to send the order to the insurance company.

Understanding Your Court Order (QDRO)

Writing the Court Order

Court orders and property settlement agreements are usually written by the lawyers representing the husband and wife before the order is given to the judge for approval and signing. A plan run by a large company may have its own model QDRO for your lawyer to use in writing the court order. Your lawyer should ask if the plan has such a model so as to get an idea of what the plan considers acceptable. You should know, however, that the plan's model court order is likely to be drawn up for the convenience of the plan rather than of an ex-wife, and may not mention all the payment options that the law permits a former spouse.

Sometimes, plan officials may be willing to look over a copy of a proposed domestic relations court order. This makes it possible for lawyers to find out in advance whether plan officials might object to certain provisions.

What Makes an Order "Qualified"?

Under the private pension law, a court order is "qualified" when it specifies the following information:

- The names and addresses of the employee and of the "alternate payee" (in this case, you),

- The name of the plan,

- Either the amount you are to be paid or the way the amount is to be figured,

- The form of payment you are to receive (for example, lifetime monthly payment, widow's pension, or lump sum), and

- When payments are to start and stop.

The court order must also meet the restrictions on the payment of benefits described earlier in this chapter. (*See* "Your Rights While Your Ex-husband Is Living," page 70, and "Your Rights After Your Ex-husband Dies," page 75.)

What to Do With Your Court Order

You or your lawyer should send an official copy of your domestic relations court order to the plan administrator, who will decide whether the order is qualified. (The plan administrator may choose another plan official or the plan's lawyer to handle the court order.)

Send your court order to the plan as soon as possible, even if the pension share isn't to be paid until years later. Your rights are not protected unless and until the plan receives your order.

Note: If your ex-husband worked under a union contract, be sure to send your court order to the *plan,* not the *union.* Although his plan may have been negotiated by the union, the pension plan is a separate organization from the union.

The plan administrator must notify promptly both the employee and the former wife that the order has been received, and send them each a copy of the plan's written procedures for determining whether a court order is qualified. (Every pension plan must have these procedures in writing.) The plan then has a "reasonable" time to decide whether the order is qualified. The law does not say what period of time is reasonable, but you should probably allow up to 90 days for the plan's decision.

By law, the plan *must* obey a domestic relations court order that *is* qualified. The plan *cannot* obey a court order that *is not* qualified.

If the Plan Rejects Your Court Order

If the plan says the court order is not qualified because, for example, it is unclear about the amount to be paid, you may have to go back to court to get the order changed. Whether you can get the order changed will depend on state law and the court.

If you disagree with the plan administrator's decision, you may appeal through the plan's "claims review" procedures. If you still cannot resolve your disagreement, then your lawyer may take the plan to court to settle your dispute. The plan *must* accept as "qualified" a court order that the court decides meets the requirements of the pension law.

While You Wait for a Decision

While the plan is determining whether the order is qualified, the plan must withhold your share of the benefits for up to 18 months from the time your payments are supposed to start. When a domestic relations court order meets all the legal requirements without having to be corrected, then a plan administrator can and should decide the order is qualified long before the 18 months have expired.

Once the court order is approved, you must be paid the withheld benefits. Since the 18-month limit only starts running from the first date you were to be paid under the order, there is little chance time will expire unless benefits were scheduled to start right after your divorce *and* you run into a big disagreement over whether the court order is qualified.

If the 18-month withholding period expired before your order was accepted, then the plan would go ahead and pay your ex-husband the withheld benefits. The plan would only give you a share of the benefits paid out to him after the QDRO is approved. But you might still have a claim to the money that had been withheld. You should ask the court to order your ex-husband to pay you the money himself, or to order the plan to add the amount to your share of his future pension benefits (although this would mean getting a change in your QDRO).

If you are divorced but there has been a delay with your QDRO, you should ask your lawyer how your benefits (including your survivor rights) can be protected. Some plans will start withholding the former spouse's share if they receive a *proposed* QDRO from either spouse.

Old Court Orders

The QDRO requirements apply to domestic relations orders issued on or after January 1, 1985 (even if the divorce was earlier). A plan already paying a former spouse her pension share on that date based on an order issued earlier *must* treat the order as a QDRO and keep paying as the order provides.

If a plan has not already started paying on a pre-1985 court order, then the plan administrator *may* treat it as a QDRO. He or she is likely to do so if the order is specific enough for the plan administrator to understand what is to be paid. However, the law does not require a plan to accept a pre-1985 order.

If you were divorced before 1985, and your divorce decree or property settlement says you are to have a certain share of the pension, you should see a lawyer about asking the court to issue a new QDRO based on your old decree.

The Role of the Department of Labor and the IRS

Both the U.S. Department of Labor and the Internal Revenue Service have the authority to issue regulations on QDROs. To date, the Labor Department has issued no regulations. Some regulations on QDROs and survivor annuities have been issued by the IRS.

Getting Information

The law provides that a wife, widow, or a divorced wife with a QDRO is a plan *beneficiary* with the right to certain pension plan information. As a practical matter, a *wife* will usually have great difficulty convincing plan officials to give her information about her husband's pension plan unless he agrees to the plan's release of information. Once your divorce proceedings begin, however, your lawyer may request information from the plan administrator, the person with the legal responsibility to provide information to plan members and beneficiaries. Your lawyer may want to request copies of certain documents that every plan must provide. These include:

Summary Plan Description. A booklet that summarizes the plan rules and tells how benefits are figured and when they are payable. Since the booklet may be as much as five years out of date without violating the law, your lawyer should also ask for a summary of any "material modifications" of the plan made after the booklet was printed.

Pension Plan Document. The legal document that is the complete set of plan rules. The plan document is usually long and hard to understand, but it is important that your lawyer have it.

Individual Benefit Statement. A paper that shows whether a worker is vested and how much in benefits he has earned thus far.* An individual benefit statement from a pension plan will usually show the benefit amount as a monthly pension starting at age 65.

---

* If your husband is already receiving benefits, then your lawyer should instead ask the plan the amount of his pension and the name of the type of payment he is receiving, such as a "Qualified Joint and Survivor Annuity."

Full Annual Financial Report. A report filed with the government every year (or every third year, in the case of a plan with fewer than 100 members). It can be useful in divorce proceedings if your husband is a company owner. For example, it will tell you how much money is in the plan. Plans also provide Summary Annual Reports that summarize this information. However, you should be sure to ask for the detailed report, called a Form 5500 (or for small plans, a Form 5500-CR).

All of these documents can be obtained from the plan administrator. A plan administrator must respond within 30 days to a written request for documents from a plan beneficiary (as well as from a plan member or retiree). You have the right to bring a lawsuit against the administrator and ask the court to fine the administrator up to $100 a day, payable to you, for every day that he or she goes over the 30-day deadline. If you win such a lawsuit, you can also ask the court to have the plan pay your attorney's fees.

The summary plan description and the plan's financial reports can also be obtained from:

Public Disclosure Room, Room N-5507
Pension and Welfare Benefits Administration
U.S. Department of Labor
200 Constitution Ave., N.W.
Washington, DC 20210
(202) 523-8771

There is a charge of 10 cents per page for copying these documents.

If your husband's pension plan covers 25 or more employees, you or your lawyer can obtain a copy of the complete plan document from the Internal Revenue Service under the Freedom of Information Act. The request should be made to the IRS Key District Office that serves the area where the pension plan office is located.

CHAPTER 3

INDIVIDUAL RETIREMENT ACCOUNTS

Taxes and Your IRA

Taxes

Money that the IRA account earns each year is not taxable until it is withdrawn from the account. When money is withdrawn from an IRA, it is not only taxable as regular income, but is also subject to tax penalties if withdrawn before the individual is age 59 1/2. But tax penalties for early withdrawals don't apply if the individual is disabled, if the money is withdrawn in the form of an *annuity*, or if it is transferred to a former spouse under the rules described in the following pages. A person *must* start withdrawing funds from his or her IRA by age 70 1/2, or pay a large penalty tax on the funds that should have been withdrawn.

Note: Withdrawing funds in the form of an annuity may allow you to take out all your money within as few as five years without a penalty, depending on your age. Contact the IRS for more information on this subject.

INDIVIDUAL RETIREMENT ACCOUNTS

Millions of employees have money in Individual Retirement Accounts (IRAs). These are retirement savings plans that employees set up at financial institutions. Most IRAs consist entirely of money that employees pay in for themselves. An IRA can be a significant asset in a divorce, especially if it is a couple's only retirement plan. This is why you need to know what your rights are if an IRA is part of your divorce.

How Individual Retirement Accounts Work

An Individual Retirement Account may be set up at a financial institution such as a bank, mutual fund, insurance company, credit union, or brokerage firm. Rules for IRAs are enforced by the Internal Revenue Service.

Personal Contributions

An *employee* who has earnings from employment or self-employment can deposit in an IRA up to *$2000* a year or an amount equal to 100 percent of his pay, whichever is less. A *two-earner couple* may each contribute $2000 to their own separate IRAs. A *one-earner couple* may contribute up to a total of *$2250* a year to two separate accounts, one for each spouse. The $2250 may be divided between the two accounts in any way as long as no more than $2000 goes into one account. Annual contributions to an IRA are fully tax deductible unless, in that year, an employee was a member of an employee pension plan *and* had an income over a certain level. The same deduction rules apply to both husband and wife even if only one member of a married couple was working under a pension plan. But the fact that your husband worked under a pension plan will not affect *your* tax deduction for your own IRA if you and your husband file separate tax returns and did not live together at any time during the year.

An IRA can be used to hold other retirement funds as well. Even if an employee has never made contributions himself, he may have an Individual Retirement Account if his employer made contributions to a Simplified Employee Pension Plan (SEP) on his behalf, or if he received money in a lump sum from a pension plan and rolled it over into an IRA.

SEP Plan

A Simplified Employee Pension Plan is an arrangement by which an employer, and sometimes employees, put retirement contributions into an IRA for each employee. An employer may pay in annually up to 15 percent of pay for each employee covered by a SEP (but no more than $22,500 in 1994, with the maximum amount increasing each year thereafter).

Pension Plan Rollover

An employee may also have money in an IRA that was paid out as a lump sum payment from his pension plan. Transferring, or "rolling over," the lump sum into an IRA allows an individual to avoid having to pay taxes on the lump sum in the year that it is received.

Receiving a SEP contribution or a lump sum rollover in a particular year does not count toward the $2000 personal IRA contribution that a worker is otherwise eligible to make.

Your Rights as a Divorced Wife

While Your Ex-husband Is Living

All or a part of an IRA may be treated as marital property at divorce and divided between husband and wife. Usually, withdrawing or transferring IRA funds to another person would mean that the owner of the IRA would have to pay taxes on the withdrawn amount in that year. But there is a way you can receive money from an IRA without the tax problem. There is a special exception under the law allowing the owner of an IRA to make a nontaxable transfer of all or a portion of an IRA to a former spouse under a court decree of divorce, or under another "written instrument incident to the divorce." The decree may be, but does not have to be, a Qualified Domestic Relations Order. (*See* Chapter 2, "Private Pensions," page 65.)

Transferring a Pension Share to an IRA

If you receive a lump sum share of your ex-husband's private pension benefits under a Qualified Domestic Relations Order, you may be able to make a tax-free rollover to your own IRA within 60 days of receiving the amount. The pension plan that pays you the lump sum is supposed to give you a notice about your right to put the money into an IRA.

Similarly, if your ex-husband is eligible to withdraw all of his pension benefits at the time you want to receive your share, he can roll over his benefits into his IRA and then sign over a part of this IRA to you (typically as a single sum).

Making Your Own Contributions

You don't always need to have earnings of your own in order to make yearly contributions to your personal IRA. Your contributions can be based on alimony or "separate maintenance" that you collect under a decree of divorce or separate maintenance.

After Your Ex-husband Dies

Whether married or single, the owner of an IRA may name anyone to receive the money left in his account upon his death. There is no legal requirement that the IRA be left to the wife or former wife. Neither the worker nor the financial institution that holds the IRA must obey a divorce court order requiring that a former wife be made the beneficiary. Your ex-husband may *voluntarily* name you to receive these funds, but he can change the name of the beneficiary at any time permitted by the financial institution holding the account.

If he is willing to provide you with survivor protection, here is one possibility you might want to consider. At retirement, many people use the amount in their IRA to buy a life annuity from an insurance company. The annuity guarantees that the retiree will receive a monthly income for as long as he lives. Rather than buying an annuity for his lifetime only, the worker can agree that when he retires he will buy a "joint and survivor" annuity that will pay benefits for his life and, after his death, benefits to a survivor. The annuity could be set up to provide you a monthly widow's benefit equal to as much as 100 percent of the pension he receives during his lifetime. Of course, this would mean that the benefits your husband receives during his lifetime would be smaller.

On the other hand, depending on the circumstances of your divorce, you may feel better protected if you ask that a share of the IRA be transferred to you as soon as possible rather than depend on your ex-husband to take action later. This would allow you to invest the money as you choose, which might include buying an insurance annuity for your own life.

Getting Information

In order to get information about your husband's IRA from the financial institution holding the account, you will usually need either a court order or your husband's written permission.

CHAPTER 4

The Federal Civil Service Retirement System

See also Appendix: Federal Employees Retirement System, p. 194

THE FEDERAL CIVIL SERVICE
RETIREMENT SYSTEM

How the Civil Service Retirement System Works

The federal Civil Service Retirement System (CSRS) covers most civilian employees of the United States government (including Postal Service employees) who were hired before 1984.* This retirement system is run by the U.S. Office of Personnel Management (OPM). Civil service retirees and their survivors typically receive lifetime monthly benefits called "annuities."

Both the employee and the government pay into the Civil Service Retirement System. However, the monthly annuity an employee receives is based on the number of years he worked and his average earnings, not on how much money was paid in. An employee who leaves the government before retirement age may choose to withdraw his own contributions and give up the right to collect an annuity later. His contributions are refunded without interest if he has worked at least five years.

An employee who works a minimum of five years under CSRS will be eligible for an annuity starting at age 62. An employee ordinarily may collect an annuity before age 62 only if he has 30 years of service and works up to age 55, or has 20 years of service and works up to age 60. (Generally, an employee whose job is abolished may retire at age 50 or over with 20 years of service, or at any age with 25 years of

---

* Most federal civilian employees hired in 1984 or after are covered by the Federal Employees Retirement System (FERS). Employees hired before 1984 were allowed to switch to FERS coverage if they did so by December 31, 1987. Certain small groups of federal employees are covered under other federal retirement systems, such as the Foreign Service Retirement and Disability System. (*See* Chapter 7.)

service.) An employee who leaves government service before retirement age must wait until age 62 to collect an annuity.*

A disabled employee with at least five years of service may start collecting a disability retirement annuity at any age. An employee with a job-related illness or injury may choose to collect federal workers' compensation instead of disability retirement.

The annuities paid to retirees and their survivors generally receive cost of living increases each year.

IMPORTANT: An employee is *not* covered by social security while he is working under the Civil Service Retirement System.

Civil Service Retirement Benefits for Divorced Wives

Federal law permits a divorced wife to receive a share of her ex-husband's civil service retirement and survivor benefits. But whether you actually receive a share and how much you receive depends on the laws of the state in which you divorce and the divorce agreement worked out between you and your ex-husband. It is very important for you also to read *Part Two*, "State Divorce Law and Your Pension Rights: Questions You Need to Answer," in this book.

*Since April 1, 1987, employees covered by the Civil Service Retirement System have also been allowed to contribute to the federal Thrift Savings Plan. This plan is separate from CSRS and is discussed in the Appendix on page 195.

Your Rights While Your Ex-husband Is Living

If you divorce, a court may award you a portion of the retirement benefit your husband receives or will receive.

In 1978, federal law was clarified to say that a state divorce court may treat a civil service retirement annuity as marital property or as a source of alimony or child support. This law also applies to *disability* annuities paid to disabled retirees.

In addition, courts were given the right to provide through a court order for the Office of Personnel Management to pay a former spouse her share of the annuity directly. The special rules and procedures for getting direct payment are discussed below.

Court Orders That Require Direct Payment

If you want to receive your share of the annuity directly from OPM rather than from your ex-husband, you need a *court order acceptable for processing*. This is an order that provides for OPM to pay you directly and that meets certain other legal requirements. (*See* "What Your Court Order Should Say," page 113.)

Under the Civil Service Retirement System, a "court order" means a final divorce decree, a court-approved property settlement or separation agreement, or some other order related to a divorce, annulment, or separation.

If your husband is still working at the time you are divorced, the divorce court can issue an order that will provide for payments to you upon his retirement. The court order should specify that payments are to be made to you by OPM, out of your ex-husband's federal retirement annuity. Specifying that OPM, rather than your former husband, is to make the payments assures you that payments will be sent regularly.

The court order must be specific about how much you are to be paid and for how long. Your benefits will be paid as a share of your former husband's benefits. The payments are made each month. You can receive payment for as long as the retiree lives, if the order so provides. (The same court order may also provide you a survivor annuity - a separate benefit - after he dies.) (*See* "Your Rights After Your Ex-husband Dies," page 103.)

Federal law allows a court to award you 100 percent of your former husband's total annuity. But OPM will pay directly to you a share equal to no more than 100 percent of his net annuity. (*See below*.) The court could award you more than the net annuity but you would have to collect the rest of your share from your ex-husband rather than from OPM. Of course, this doesn't mean you are likely to be awarded 100 percent of the total or net annuity. The court will look to state law to decide how much your share will be.

The *net* annuity is the amount your ex-husband receives after certain deductions are made. These deductions can include:

- The cost of premiums for the retiree's life and health insurance and Medicare.

- Withholding for the retiree's federal income tax.

- Money the retiree owes the government.

- Annuity reductions taken to provide a survivor annuity, for you or someone else.

OPM will not pay you any portion of the annuity that is being paid to another former wife under an earlier court order.

Your Rights After Your Ex-husband Dies

Once your ex-husband dies, your share of his lifetime annuity stops. However, you may be entitled to a *former spouse survivor annuity.*

Until the Civil Service Retirement Spouse Equity Act of 1984 (Spouse Equity Act) went into effect on May 7, 1985, a former wife could not collect a regular survivor annuity. But now, a *former spouse survivor annuity* may be provided for a divorced wife in one of two ways: through a court order or through the ex-husband's *voluntary election.* (A former spouse may also receive a different type of survivor annuity known as an *insurable interest annuity.*)

The *former spouse survivor annuity* is really the same monthly benefit you would have received if you had remained married, but the rules for getting a survivor annuity as a *former* spouse are more complicated. A former spouse survivor annuity can be paid to a divorced widow of an employee who dies while he is working for the federal government or after he starts collecting his annuity.

Once the employee retires, he pays for part of the cost of a survivor annuity through a reduction in his own annuity. No more than the amount of one "spouse" survivor annuity can be paid. If the retiree has a current wife, or more than one former wife when he dies, the survivor annuity can be paid all to one person, or divided between two or more widows.

You can receive a former spouse survivor annuity in addition to any annuity you may be receiving through your own work.

If Your Ex-husband Dies Before Retirement

Rules for Getting a Former Spouse Survivor Annuity

If a federal worker dies while still employed by the federal government, his divorced wife may be eligible for a former spouse survivor annuity. Your ex-husband must have worked at least 18 months under the Civil Service Retirement System and you must have an "acceptable" court order awarding you the survivor annuity. (*See* "Acceptable Court Order," page 109.) There is no cost to the employee to protect his ex-wife if he dies while he is still employed; that is, the amount of his future annuity is not affected. Your former spouse survivor annuity is 55 percent of the annuity your ex-husband had earned at the time of his death. Your benefits start immediately after your former husband's death and continue monthly for your life, unless you remarry before age 55. (*See* "How Remarriage May Affect Your Survivor Annuity," page 112.) Only an acceptable court order will protect your rights. Your ex-husband cannot make a voluntary election to provide you a benefit if he dies *while still employed.*

A Gap in Survivor Protection: *If a federal worker dies after leaving federal employment, but before reaching retirement age (usually age 62), no annuity is payable to any survivor.* OPM will, however, pay to a *beneficiary* a lump sum refund of the worker's contributions, plus interest. You can be eligible for this special type of lump sum only if your ex-husband named you as beneficiary on a government form given to him by his personnel office.

If he did name you as a beneficiary during your marriage or after your divorce, you will remain the beneficiary unless and until your ex-husband removes your name. If he listed no one as beneficiary, then the lump sum is automatically payable to a close relative of his, but not to a former wife. OPM will not honor a court order requiring that this lump sum be paid to you.

For you as a divorced wife, your ex-husband's death during this period means that, although you can receive part of his contributions if you are named as the beneficiary, *you lose the right* to a future share of his annuity and to your survivor annuity.

If your husband is some years from retirement age and he has left the government or might leave before retirement age, then think about negotiating a provision in your property settlement saying that if he does leave the government he will get private life insurance to give you a benefit equal to the civil service survivor annuity.

If Your Ex-husband Dies After Retirement

Rules for Getting a Former Spouse Survivor Annuity

If your ex-husband dies after starting to collect his annuity, a former spouse survivor annuity may be payable to you through an *acceptable court order* or through your ex-husband's *voluntary election*. It starts immediately after the retiree's death and continues for your lifetime unless you remarry before age 55. (*See* "How Remarriage May Affect Your Survivor Annuity," page 112.)

How Will Your Benefits Be Figured?

The maximum former spouse survivor annuity is equal to 55 percent of the retiree's annuity before any reductions. In order for you to receive the former spouse survivor annuity, your ex-husband normally must accept a reduction in his own annuity.

■ Example

Here's how it works:

Melvin is eligible for an annuity of $1000 a month before any reductions. But since his ex-wife Dorothy has a court order giving her a survivor annuity, Melvin's benefit will be automatically reduced. The reduction is equal to 2 1/2 percent of the first $300 a month plus 10 percent of the rest of his benefit. In Melvin's case, the reduction comes out to $77.50, leaving him with a benefit of $922.50.

$1000 − [(2 1/2 % of $300) + (10% of $700)] = Melvin's monthly annuity

$1000 − [$7.50 + $70] = Melvin's monthly annuity

$1000 − [$77.50] = $922.50

If he dies first, his ex-wife Dorothy will receive a former spouse survivor annuity of $550 a month, which is 55 percent of $1000.

55% of $1000 = Dorothy's monthly survivor annuity

55% of $1000 = $550

Let's say that Melvin is thinking about remarrying and will agree to give Dorothy only half the survivor annuity. In this case, the reduction would only be based on half of Melvin's annuity, or $500. The reduction amount is then subtracted from his full annuity, which is $1000.

$1000 − [(2 1/2% of $300) + (10% of $200)] = Melvin's monthly annuity

$1000 − [$7.50 + $20] = Melvin's monthly annuity

$1000 − [$27.50] = $972.50

After Melvin dies, Dorothy will receive a monthly survivor annuity equal to 55 percent of $500, or $275.

55% of $500 = Dorothy's monthly survivor annuity

55% of $500 = $275

Note: If Dorothy dies first or remarries before age 55, Melvin can resume collecting his unreduced annuity or name his new wife to receive the survivor annuity.

Negotiating the Survivor Annuity

A civil service survivor annuity can be an extremely valuable benefit to a former wife, but is sometimes difficult to secure in a divorce. If your ex-husband strongly objects to giving you all or a part of the survivor annuity because his own annuity will be reduced, be sure to remind him that it costs him nothing to provide you with a survivor annuity if he dies while still employed.

In order to have the maximum possible survivor protection in the event of his death *after* retirement, however, you may want to consider agreeing to pay for the full cost starting when your share of the annuity becomes payable. This can be done in your court order, as long as your share of your husband's lifetime annuity is at least as much as the amount of money that OPM needs to deduct for your former spouse survivor annuity. *(Con't. on next page)*

Also, your husband may object to giving you most of the survivor annuity if he is planning to remarry and wants this benefit for his new wife. At the very least, you should arrange to have the maximum available survivor annuity until the new wife meets the requirements for survivor benefits, which include being married for nine months. Your court order could provide that only at that point would you become eligible for a partial rather than a full survivor annuity.

When Your Written Consent Is Needed to Give Up the Survivor Annuity

An employee who retires after May 6, 1985, is required to get his wife's written consent before signing away any part of the survivor annuity. An employee doesn't have to get his wife's written consent if he can show OPM that she can't be located, or when a court decides that there are "exceptional circumstances" that justify not getting her consent. (OPM has rules explaining more about when these and other exceptions apply.)

If you and your husband are married when he retires, and you do not agree to give up the survivor annuity at his retirement, he can't reduce or eliminate the survivor annuity later, at least not while you are still married. He does have a second chance to sign up for or increase a survivor annuity for his current wife even if he partially or completely waived (gave up) that chance at retirement. This "second chance" election for his current wife must be made within 18 months after his retirement. However, once you give your consent for your husband to sign away the survivor annuity at retirement, you as the spouse have no legal right to have the survivor annuity option restored. *Keep in mind that a divorce court cannot award you a survivor annuity that you have previously given up.*

Whether you are in the middle of divorce negotiations or you only suspect that a divorce may be in your future, don't sign away your right to a survivor annuity in exchange for your husband's promise to give you his government life insurance (known as Federal Employees Government Life Insurance, or FEGLI). No matter what agreement you have with him - even if it's part of your court-approved property settlement - your husband has the right under federal law to name anyone as his FEGLI beneficiary, and he may remove or change the beneficiary at any time.

If you and your husband are divorced when he retires, he does not need your consent to take an annuity for his life only, unless an acceptable court order says you are to have a survivor annuity.

Ways That Survivor Protection Can Be Provided to Former Wives

This section explains the requirements for getting a former spouse survivor annuity by using an *acceptable court order* or the ex-husband's *voluntary election*. It also says how a former spouse can be eligible for an *insurable interest annuity*.

Acceptable Court Order

An acceptable court order may require your ex-husband to provide you with a former spouse survivor annuity. A court order can be used to give you survivor protection whether your former husband dies while still working or after he retires. (*Remember*: A court order is the *only* way you can be protected if he dies while still working.) The order may say that you are to receive the maximum survivor annuity of 55 percent, or it can provide a smaller benefit. If you are to receive only part of the survivor annuity, the retiree's next wife or another former wife would be eligible to receive the rest of the survivor annuity. *You can ask a divorce court to award you the survivor annuity if:*

Your divorce occurs *after* May 6, 1985, *and*

- You and your husband were married when he retired and he elected a survivor annuity for you; *or*

- Your husband retired before May 7, 1985, married you after retirement, and then elected a survivor annuity for you before May 7, 1985; *or*

- He is not yet retired.

If you were divorced *before* May 7, 1985, a court cannot order a survivor annuity for you.

Voluntary Election

The Spouse Equity Act established *voluntary election* opportunities, allowing some retirees to sign up for a full or partial survivor annuity for a former wife. Your former husband can choose to provide you with a survivor annuity by making an "election" at retirement, or after retirement, *if his post-retirement decision is made within two years after the divorce.*

Making a voluntary election requires the retiree to take a reduced annuity in the future and to repay with interest the amount that would have been withheld from his annuity had he made the same election at retirement. (Repayment is made through a reduction in the retiree's annuity over his remaining lifetime.) If the retiree has remarried by the time he makes the election for his former wife, then his current wife must give her written consent. A voluntary election for a former spouse lasts until she dies or remarries before age 55.

Remember: Your ex-husband's voluntary election protects you only if he dies *after* retirement.

IMPORTANT: If you were still married when your husband retired and you are depending on him to voluntarily keep your name on record to receive the survivor annuity, you need to know that the fact that your ex-husband continues to take a reduced annuity *is not enough* to protect your right to benefits. He must also notify OPM in writing, *within two years after your divorce*, that he wants you to receive the survivor annuity as his divorced spouse. *If he does not make this after-divorce election, you will not receive a survivor annuity.*

Special Former Spouse Survivor Annuity

The Spouse Equity Act provided special automatic former spouse survivor annuities to ex-wives of federal employees who retired (or died after becoming eligible to retire) before May 7, 1985, and who were divorced before May 8, 1987. (There were also several other requirements.) The final date to apply was May 8, 1989.

Insurable Interest Annuity

At retirement, a married or single employee may choose a reduced annuity that will pay a survivor annuity to a person with an *insurable interest* in the retiree. The person could be a current or former spouse, a retiree's child (minor or adult), or other close relative. This survivor annuity can only be provided by an employee who is in good health, and is not available to an employee retiring on disability. The insurable interest annuity is a benefit separate from a current or former spouse survivor annuity. It is a voluntary option for the retiree. A court can't order it to be paid, and OPM will not honor a court order awarding an insurable interest annuity to an ex-wife or anyone else.

The maximum insurable interest annuity is equal to 55 percent of the retiree's annuity *after* the reduction for the insurable interest. (The former spouse survivor annuity is 55 percent of the retiree's annuity *before* any reduction.) The insurable interest annuity will not be reduced by any other deductions in the retiree's annuity, even a survivor annuity for a current spouse. The exact amount of the reduction, which can range from 10 percent to 40 percent, depends on the age of the named beneficiary compared to the age of the retiree.

Instead of having your former husband provide you a regular former spouse survivor annuity, you and he may agree that he will provide you with an insurable interest survivor annuity. This could be to your advantage as a former wife, because it is payable for as long as you live, *even if you remarry*.

Its disadvantage is that it costs the retiree more, and results in a smaller benefit for you than the regular survivor annuity. It is also less protected than a former spouse survivor annuity. If your former husband fails to live up to his agreement to make the election, you will have no recourse except to take him (or his estate, if he has died) to court. Also, even if he has chosen the insurable interest annuity for you, he may later cancel the benefit if he remarries and wants to provide a current spouse survivor annuity for his new wife. The insurable interest annuity cannot be transferred to another person.

A divorced employee who has remarried before he retires could take a reduction at retirement to provide a regular survivor annuity for his former wife and take an additional reduction for the insurable interest for his current wife, or vice versa.

How Remarriage May Affect Your Survivor Annuity

If you remarry before age 55, your right to a former spouse survivor annuity is *permanently* ended. The remarriage penalty applies to a court-ordered or voluntary survivor annuity. Remarriage at age 55 or after doesn't affect your rights to any of these benefits, nor does remarriage *at any age* affect your right to an insurable interest survivor annuity.

If your ex-husband remarries, your former spouse survivor annuity is not reduced or eliminated unless your court order says it is. His new wife will be eligible to receive only the remaining portion, if any, of the survivor annuity. But if your portion of the survivor annuity stops being paid because of *your* death or remarriage, then his new wife can start receiving your share.

If You Die First

If you die before your former husband, your share of the annuity doesn't necessarily end. Unless your court order provides otherwise, the remaining share will be paid to him. Although state law may have something to say about what happens to your share of the annuity after your death, this issue is usually negotiable between the spouses. Federal regulations permit a court order to provide that your share be paid to a child of the government retiree or to your estate.

Note: You may want to consider offering to let your husband keep his entire annuity if *you* die first, as long as you get to have the entire *survivor* annuity if *he* dies first.

If you die after your former husband had already retired with a reduced annuity that was to provide a survivor annuity to you, he may ask OPM to eliminate the reduction in his annuity or he may keep the reduction to provide a survivor annuity to his new spouse, if he has remarried. As a former spouse, you cannot transfer your survivor annuity to someone else.

What Your Court Order Should Say

OPM has issued detailed guidelines explaining how a court order can be written so that you can get the share of your ex-husband's annuity and survivor annuity that you and he agree upon. The regulations also contain model paragraphs that can be used in writing court orders. Your lawyer should be aware that the rules for civil service annuity court orders are very different from the rules for pension court orders under other retirement systems. The regulations are available in the following government booklet:

A Handbook for Attorneys on Court-ordered Retirement and Health Benefits Under the Civil Service Retirement System, the Federal Employees Retirement System, and the Federal Employees Health Benefits Program, (Pub. No. S/N/006-000-01377-5), available from the U.S. Government Printing Office. It may be ordered by mail for $13.00 by writing:

> New Orders
> Superintendent of Documents
> P.O. Box 371954
> Pittsburgh, PA 15250-7954

Make Sure That Your Court Order Protects Your Benefits

You could lose out on your court-ordered benefits if your ex-husband leaves his job before retirement age and withdraws all his own contributions. That is because no annuity is payable to the employee or spouse once the employee contributions are withdrawn.

Before an employee may withdraw his contributions, he must give official written notice of the withdrawal to both his current wife and his former wife (if the divorce took place after May 6, 1985). However, you as the former wife do not have an automatic right to prevent the withdrawal or to claim a share of the refunded contributions.

To protect your rights, keep this in mind: OPM says that an employee will *not* be permitted to voluntarily withdraw his contributions before retirement if OPM has received a domestic relations court order with a provision that "expressly relates" to the lump sum refund, and payment of the lump sum at that time would erase the former wife's annuity rights provided in the court order. OPM doesn't explain this rule further but if you are getting a divorce before your husband's retirement, *the court order that gives you a share of the annuity or the survivor annuity should also say that he is not to withdraw his contributions.* Or, the court order can provide that if he does make a withdrawal, you will be paid a share of the refunded amount. (But remember that your *annuity* rights will end once he withdraws this money.)

If your ex-husband has not yet applied for his annuity, but you have a court order giving you a share of his benefits, look to see whether the order also says that he is not to withdraw his contributions before retirement. If the court order does *not* have this language, check with your lawyer to find out whether you should have the order changed to include this provision.

Note: If your court order neglects to say that your ex-husband is not to withdraw his contributions, and you later discover that he did take out the money without notifying you in writing first, OPM says that you still may be able to get a share of his benefits. Among other things, you need to prove to OPM that your ex-husband committed fraud by signing your name on the required "notice-to-spouse" form or that he falsely claimed to OPM that he didn't know where you were living (and therefore couldn't send you the notice). If this happens to you, be sure to get the advice of a lawyer about what to do.

What to Do With Your Court Order

Once you have the court order, you or your lawyer should send an official copy, certified by the court clerk, to the following address:

Office of Personnel Management
Retirement & Insurance Group
P.O. Box 17
Washington, DC 20044

Providing Information to OPM

Along with the court order, send a signed and dated letter giving:

- Your name, address, and social security number
- Your ex-husband's name, address, and social security number
- His date of birth
- His civil service claim number (if he's already retired)

You also need to state in the letter that the court order has not been "amended, superseded, or set aside," (that is, changed).

Is the Order "Acceptable"?

Once OPM receives your court order, it will decide whether it is a *court order acceptable for processing*, meaning that the order meets specific legal requirements.

If the Order Is Acceptable

If OPM says the court order is *acceptable*, it will send you a letter saying how it will figure your share of the annuity and the survivor annuity (if one is awarded). If your former husband has already retired, OPM will also tell you how much you will be getting and when payments start.

OPM will notify your former husband that it plans to make payments to you out of his annuity, and will send him a copy of the order. He can prevent payment to you only if he obtains and sends to OPM a new court order that invalidates the order that you sent. Of course, this does not necessarily mean that a court would grant him such an order, especially if you do not consent to it.

Even if OPM says that your order is acceptable, you may disagree with its interpretation of the wording of the order. If you cannot convince OPM to accept your reading of the order, you may have to go back to court for a new order that clarifies the previous order.

Note: If you believe that you were awarded a survivor annuity as well as a share of the annuity during your former husband's lifetime, make sure that OPM's letter also mentions the survivor annuity. If it does not, then you should write back to request that the agency confirm that you are to have a survivor benefit. It is important to know as soon as possible whether OPM thinks that the wording of your court order is adequate for this purpose. Otherwise, your order may need to be revised to comply with OPM's requirements. (*But see* "Timing Can Be Crucial," page 117.)

If the Order Is Not Acceptable

If OPM says that your order is not acceptable, it will give the reasons why. For example, if your order required OPM to pay your share of the annuity starting immediately, but your former husband was still working, the order would be rejected because OPM will not pay a former spouse until the employee starts receiving his annuity. You would have to go back to court to get a revised order that provided that your payments were to begin when your former husband retired.

Timing Can Be Crucial

Remember, it is essential to mail an official copy of your court order to OPM *as soon as possible after the divorce.* This is especially true if your ex-husband is close to retirement and your court order requires your ex-husband to select a certain retirement option. Timing can be particularly important if your court order is issued after your divorce and provides for a survivor annuity. OPM will not accept a court order for a survivor annuity if:

- The order is issued *after* your ex-husband's death (*See* Example 1),

OR

- The order is issued *after* your ex-husband retires, *and* it is a "modification" of an earlier divorce decree, court order, or court-approved property settlement. (*See* Example 2.)

These restrictions can be devastating for a divorced wife. Here are two situations in which you could end up with an unacceptable court order and no survivor annuity.

■ Example 1: Court order issued after ex-husband's death.

You and your husband divorce while he's still working. The court agrees that you are entitled to receive a portion of his annuity and the former spouse survivor annuity, but tells you to come back to court when he is ready to retire and apply for his annuity so that the court can figure the exact amount of your benefits. Several years later your ex-husband dies suddenly, before reaching retirement age. Even if the court then agreed to issue the order awarding the former spouse annuity, OPM would reject the order as being issued after your ex-husband's death, and you will not get a survivor annuity.

■ Example 2: Court order issued after ex-husband's retirement.

You and your husband divorce after he retires. You both agree that you should receive the former spouse survivor annuity, but the court order mistakenly fails to mention the survivor annuity. Getting the court to fix the mistake and issue a corrected order is easy, but OPM will reject the second order as being an amendment or clarification of an order issued after your ex-husband's retirement.

OPM will eventually start making some exceptions to this very strict rule about modified court orders that award survivor annuities, allowing certain minor changes in orders following a divorce, even if they are made after the employee retires.

For the time being, you can help protect yourself by making sure the judge signs your divorce decree *and* the necessary court order at the same time. Your lawyer should also see that the court order is written as carefully as possible so that it will not need any changes after it is signed.

If you cannot persuade OPM to accept your revised order, then you should try to convince your former husband to make a voluntary election for a survivor annuity. (*See* page 110.)

Note: If the court order awarding you a survivor annuity is issued part of a *bifurcated* (or two-step) divorce, OPM will probably accept the court order even though it is technically issued after the divorce. (*See* pages 36-37 on bifurcated divorces.)

Getting Information

If you or your lawyer would like to make a rough estimate of the benefits your husband may be entitled to receive, various companies publish inexpensive books on the Civil Service Retirement System that include charts to help you figure the amount of your husband's benefits. Some federal agencies will give employees an individual estimate of their benefits. An employee also has the right to request an estimate from OPM.

Your husband can sign a consent form so that you or your lawyer can get information about his retirement benefits. Or, as part of the divorce proceedings, you can ask the court to order your husband's retirement records from OPM, or from his agency personnel office (if he has not started collecting his annuity). At most, the government will only tell you the amount of the employee's own contributions and the estimated or actual monthly amount of the annuity; it will not figure the total lump sum value of the annuity.

OPM's Retirement Information Office has information on a variety of retirement-related topics. The number is (202) 606-0500, although you will have to wait on hold if you want to speak to a person rather than listen to recordings. To get the most up-to-date information about your rights as a former wife, you should contact OPM rather than your ex-husband's agency personnel office, or order the booklet on page 113.

CHAPTER 5

THE MILITARY RETIREMENT SYSTEM

THE MILITARY RETIREMENT SYSTEM

How the Military Retirement System Works

The military retirement system covers members of the uniformed services, such as the Army, Air Force, Navy, Marines, Coast Guard, the Reserves, and the National Guard. It also includes commissioned officers of the Public Health Service and the National Oceanic and Atmospheric Administration. People working under the military retirement system are called "*military members*." The retirement system is run by the U.S. Department of Defense. Each major military branch has its own finance center which is responsible for handling retirement applications and paying checks to retirees and family members.

A military member with 20 years of service has the right to collect a lifetime monthly pension, called "*retired pay*," as soon as he leaves the service. A member who becomes disabled may become eligible for "*disability retired pay*," even if he does not have 20 years. A member of the Reserves or the National Guard must have 20 years of "creditable" service and be at least age 60 to retire. The federal government pays for these benefits; military members are not required to pay into the system (although they do pay into social security as do non-military workers).

If a military retiree is disabled, part or all of his retired pay may be replaced by disability retired pay or disability compensation paid by the Department of Veterans Affairs (formerly the Veterans Administration).

Military retirees and their survivors receive periodic cost of living increases in their monthly benefits.

Military Retirement Benefits for Divorced Wives

Most of the pension protections for military ex-wives were established through the Uniformed Services Former Spouses' Protection Act of 1982 (USFSPA). This law was passed to overrule a United States Supreme Court 1981 case, *McCarty* v. *McCarty*, saying that military retired pay could *not* be treated as marital property at divorce. USFSPA allows a state divorce court to award you a share of your ex-husband's retired pay as marital property. The state court order can say that you will receive a share of the retired pay while he is living and a survivor benefit after he dies. The law also provides other benefits for military ex-wives, such as health insurance.

Your Rights While Your Ex-husband Is Living

USFSPA generally *permits,* but does not require, a state divorce court to award you a share of retired pay. It is up to the court, relying on state law, to first decide whether you will get a share, either as marital property or alimony.* The court must then take into account what USFSPA says about dividing military retired pay. USFSPA also allows you to negotiate a share of the retired pay as part of your property settlement.

Your payments may be paid by your former husband or by the military retirement system. In order for you to receive payment directly from the military, the court award (or property settlement) must be in the form of a court order that meets certain rules. The rules for getting direct payment of a share of retired pay are set by USFSPA. (*See* "Direct Payment of Your Share of Retired Pay," page 126.)

---

* In this chapter on The Military Retirement System, "alimony" is used to mean support payments, not an award of property.

Court Jurisdiction Requirements

In order for a state divorce court to divide up any type of pension, or order alimony or child support, it must have legal authority, known as "jurisdiction," over the person with the pension. A court gets this type of jurisdiction when that person either files for divorce himself, or is "served with process," that is, given formal notice of a divorce lawsuit filed by his wife that orders him to appear in that court. Each state has its own jurisdiction rules.

To treat military retired pay as marital property, the court must also have "special jurisdiction." The federal USFSPA law that requires this special jurisdiction makes it more difficult, and sometimes impossible, for a former military wife to get a share of the retired pay as marital property. (This rule does not have to be met to get a share of retired pay as alimony or child support.) A court has special jurisdiction, or the authority to treat the retired pay as marital property, *only if the military member or retiree:*

- *"Resides," that is, lives, in that court's jurisdiction, other than by reason of his military assignment.* For example, if he lives in Maryland because he chooses to, not only because he's been assigned to that location, then federal law would say that he is within a Maryland divorce court's jurisdiction. (Only an active duty member would have a "military assignment.")

OR

- *Has his "domicile," or permanent home, within the state over which the court has authority.* A person may have several residences, but only one domicile. (An active duty member's domicile is likely to be the state which the military considers his "home of record.")

OR

- *Consents to the court's jurisdiction.* For example, if the military member is the one who filed for divorce in that court, that would be considered "consenting" to the court's jurisdiction for purposes of dividing the retired pay.

This rule applies in any case where the court treats retired pay as marital property, *even if you trade off your share of your ex-husband's retired pay in order to receive other marital property.*

IMPORTANT: If you are the one filing for divorce, ask your lawyer — before starting divorce proceedings — how this special jurisdiction requirement will affect your right to a share of the retired pay.

Direct Payment of Your Share of Retired Pay

A court order may provide that an ex-wife receive a share of the monthly retired pay directly from the military, to be paid at the same time it is paid to her former husband. If you want direct monthly payments from the military, your court order must meet certain requirements. (*See* "Requirements for Your Court Order," page 128.)

Note: Direct payment of alimony from the military is not available to a *separated* spouse, although you could be paid directly if your husband asks the military for a "voluntary allotment" to you out of his retired pay or wages.

How Much Can You Get?

Federal law says that a former wife can receive no more than 50 percent of a retiree's *"disposable"* retired pay through *direct payment* from the military.

What Is "Disposable Pay"?

Disposable pay is what is left of the retired pay after certain deductions. These include:

- *Survivor Benefit Reduction.* If the retiree is providing you with a survivor benefit (known as the Survivor Benefit Plan annuity), his retired pay will be reduced during his lifetime. Your share of the disposable retired pay is figured after this reduction. A reduction he takes to provide the Survivor Benefit Plan (SBP) annuity to his current wife, or anyone else, does not affect your share of the disposable retired pay.

- *Disability Benefits.* If the retiree is disabled, some or all of his retired pay will be replaced by disability benefits. To calculate the amount of disposable pay, the military finance center will subtract the disability retirement pay to which your ex-husband is entitled. They will also subtract disability compensation paid to him by the Department of Veterans Affairs (VA).

  Note: If his military disability retirement pay *increases* because he becomes more disabled after retirement, this percentage increase in disability payments will not be subtracted from the disposable retired pay before your share is figured and, therefore, will not decrease your share, if your court order is issued after November 14, 1986. (*See* "Disability Retirement Benefits," page 140.)

- *Government Pay.* If the retiree takes a civilian job with the federal government, he may have to give up (waive) part of his military retired pay while he is working. (*See* "Government Re-employment," page 144.) The portion of the retired pay that is waived is subtracted from disposable pay, and thus will reduce your share.

- *Court-martial Forfeitures.* Also subtracted from disposable retired pay are "forfeitures" imposed by a court-martial.

Note: If you were divorced before February 3, 1991, disposable pay may be further reduced. Additional

127

deductions include amounts withheld for the retiree's income taxes and debts the retiree owes the federal government.

Can You Share in "Non-Disposable" Retired Pay?

Even though a former wife can't receive more than 50 percent of the disposable pay through *direct payment,* some courts have, nevertheless, awarded former wives a portion of the "gross" retired pay that exceeds 50 percent of disposable retired pay. When the military finance center received such an order, it would go ahead and pay the former wife up to the maximum amount permitted for direct payment, but then she would have to look to her ex-husband for payment of the extra amount.

A recent law passed by Congress seems to say that in the future, a divorce court cannot include as marital property *any amounts* deducted in figuring disposable pay.

Court Orders

Requirements for Your Court Order

To get your share of the retired pay paid to you by the finance center, you need a "final court order" that meets certain requirements.

USFSPA defines "court order" as a final court decree of divorce, annulment, or legal separation, or a court-ordered or approved property settlement connected with the decree. A "final" court order is one that can't be appealed, that wasn't appealed within the time limit allowed by state law, or that was appealed but has been finally decided.

The court order needs to contain certain information, including:

- Your ex-husband's name.

- Your right to a marital property share from the retired pay, or your right to alimony or support (the order does not necessarily have to specify that the alimony or support is to be paid from the retired pay).

- The amount you are to be paid.

- The length of time you are to be paid, specifying when payments are to start and stop.

You can get *direct payment* as long as the court order contains the above information. The court order does not have to actually require the finance center to pay you. Your lawyer should be familiar with the law and regulations on court orders for direct payment, including some other minor requirements not discussed here.

Length of Marriage

To get *direct payment* of retired pay as *marital property*, you must have been married for at least 10 years of the military member's active duty service. The law does not say these have to be continuous years. So if you were married to the same husband more than once, you only need a *total* of 10 years. There is no length-of-marriage requirement for getting a share paid as *alimony or support*. There is also no length of marriage requirement for being awarded the Survivor Benefit Plan annuity.

Specifying the Amount

The amount you are to be paid must be specified in the court order either as a dollar amount, a percentage, or a fraction of the retired pay. The court order doesn't have to say you are getting a percentage or fraction of *disposable* retired pay, but the finance center will figure your share based on disposable pay.

 If the amount is stated as a percentage or fraction, you will receive a portion of future cost of living increases. If the court order states your share as a dollar amount, you will not receive cost of living adjustments unless the order also provides for them. (Court orders for alimony or support often state the amount in dollars.)

When Do Payments Start and Stop?

Payments to you may begin as soon as the retiree starts collecting his retired pay and they can continue monthly for as long as he lives. (The military doesn't pay retirement benefits in the form of a lump sum.) Payments stop when you die, or when he dies, or at an earlier date if set by court order. (After your ex-husband dies, you may be eligible for a survivor benefit.) (*See* "Your Rights After Your Ex-husband Dies," page 132.)

What to Do With Your Court Order

As soon as you are divorced and you have a court order providing you with a share of the retired pay, you or your lawyer should send a copy of your order to the military finance center for his military branch. (*See* "Where To Send..." page 146.)

You or your lawyer will need to send an official copy of the court order or decree, along with other information required by federal regulation. The copy of the court order must have been certified by the court clerk within the last 90 days. The other information you need to send includes items such as the addresses and social security numbers of you and your ex-husband, and is listed in the application form "Request for Former Spouse Payments From Retired Pay" that you can get from the military finance center. The completed form should be signed by you (not your lawyer).

Send it along with your court order, keeping copies of all materials you send. All the required materials must be sent to the finance center by certified mail or registered mail (return receipt requested), or by "personal service." If the materials are sent by any method other than one of these three ways, the finance center will not accept your documents and you will have to send everything again.

Although every finance center must follow the same law and regulations on handling court orders, the centers carry out the rules in somewhat different ways. One center may interpret the rules more strictly than another, so try to follow the rules as closely as possible.

Within 30 days after the military finance center receives all the necessary papers from you, the center will send your ex-husband a copy of the court order and information about how much and when you are to be paid. Your ex-husband can hold up your payments if, within another 30 days, he tells the military finance center that the court order is invalid for some reason. For instance, he might say that the order is not final and is being appealed in court.

If there is a dispute about the amount to be paid, as, for example, in a case where the finance center had received two conflicting orders, the center will withhold that part of the payment that is in dispute, and only pay the retiree the amount that is agreed upon as his share. The withheld amount will be paid out to the appropriate spouse once the dispute is resolved.

Notifying You

Within 90 days of receiving all your materials (assuming they were mailed in the required way), the finance center is supposed to inform you when your payments will start and how much they will be. (*Remember:* Payments to you can't start until your ex-husband starts getting his payments.) The finance center will also tell you if your court order can't be honored, and explain why. If you disagree with the decision, you may write to ask for a reconsideration. You should specify exactly what you disagree with and explain why. If your request for reconsideration is denied, then you may need to go back to court to try to get the order modified, if possible.

How Does Remarriage Affect Your Benefits?

Neither your remarriage nor your ex-husband's remarriage stops the payments from retired pay unless the court order provides for benefits to stop. A court order for alimony or support payments will often say that the ex-wife's remarriage cuts off payment. (Your remarriage *may* affect your right to the Survivor Benefit Plan annuity. *See* "How Does Remarriage Affect Your SBP Annuity?," page 139.)

Your Rights After Your Ex-husband Dies: The Survivor Benefit Plan Annuity

A divorced military wife may be able to collect a survivor benefit after her ex-husband dies. Under the military retirement system, the survivor benefit is called the *Survivor Benefit Plan (SBP) annuity.* Your rights to the SBP annuity are likely to depend on when you divorce, when your ex-husband dies, and what arrangements were made at the time of your divorce.

You may receive a survivor benefit if your former husband is either eligible for or actually receiving retired pay at the time of his death. A military member usually becomes eligible for retirement after serving 20 years on active duty.

However, getting a survivor benefit is not automatic after divorce even if you would have received the benefit if your husband had died while you were still married. *You need to make these arrangements at the time you divorce*, which usually means getting a court order or agreement. If you wait, you are likely to lose out on these benefits.

The SBP annuity can be paid to a wife or former wife, whichever the member selected, but not both at the same time. After the retiree's death, the retiree's chosen beneficiary immediately starts receiving a monthly benefit for the rest of her life. Note, however, that remarriage can affect your rights. (*See* "How Does Remarriage Affect Your SBP Annuity?," page 139.)

Your Written Consent Needed To Give Up SBP Annuity

The Survivor Benefit Plan goes into effect as soon as a married military member becomes eligible to retire. Once he actually retires, his retired pay will be automatically reduced to provide the SBP to his current wife after he dies. If he wants to provide less than the maximum SBP or none at all, he must get her written consent at the time he applies for retired pay.

The military member is not required to get his wife's consent if:

• His wife cannot be located, *or*

• Getting her consent would be "inappropriate" due to "exceptional circumstances," *or*

• The SBP annuity is being provided to a former wife. (In this case, the current wife will be notified that she will not receive the SBP annuity.)

If you are still married when your husband retires and you agree to sign away part or all of the SBP annuity, you cannot change your decision. This means that if you are later divorced, you cannot be awarded benefits that you have already given up.

Note: Members who retired before November 8, 1985, could sign away part or all of the SBP annuity without a wife's consent. The wife was only entitled to written notice that she would not be getting this benefit. If you are a former wife of a member who retired before November 8, 1985, you can't be awarded a survivor benefit that your ex-husband legally gave up while he was married to you.

How Will Your Benefit Be Figured?

If you are under age 62 when your ex-husband dies, the maximum SBP annuity you can receive will be 55 percent of his retired pay, before any reductions. At age 62, your annuity will be reduced to take into account your divorced widow social security benefit. (*See* "Automatic Reduction at Age 62," page 134.)

Note: The amount of the SBP annuity payable to a former wife is not affected if the retiree's basic retired pay was replaced by disability retired pay or VA compensation.

In order for you to get the SBP annuity, the retiree must agree to accept a reduction in his own retired pay. The reduction is 6 1/2 percent of the retired pay.* The reduction for him is less if you and he agree that you will receive less than the maximum SBP annuity.

Here's how it works:

■ Example

James is eligible for retired pay of $1000 a month. His ex-wife Jackie is eligible to receive the SBP annuity. James' benefit will be reduced as follows:

$1000 -   (6.5% of $1000)   =   James' reduced retired pay

$1000 - $65   = $935

If he dies first, before Jackie reaches age 62, she will receive:

55% of $1000   = $550

Automatic Reduction at Age 62

Your SBP annuity is automatically reduced when you reach age 62 to take into account the divorced widow social security benefit that you may be receiving at that time. However, the reduction will apply *even if* you are not collecting a social security spouse benefit.

---

* Before March 1, 1990, the reduction in monthly retired pay was 2 1/2 percent of the first $337 plus 10 percent of the rest of the retired pay.

How to Figure the Age-62 Automatic Reduction

When you reach age 62, the SBP annuity is cut from 55 percent to only 35 percent of retired pay. For example, a $550 benefit would go down to $350 a month. This works out to about a 36 percent reduction in the benefit you receive. This is called the "flat percent reduction."

Another way of figuring the SBP reduction at age 62 can be used if your ex-husband was covered by the SBP before October 2, 1985. The finance center will use the method that gives you the larger SBP annuity. This method subtracts an amount equal to your social security divorced widow benefit from your SBP annuity. To figure out how much of your social security benefit to subtract, the finance center *will* count:

- The portion of your social security divorced widow benefit that your ex-husband earned while on military active duty, and

- The social security divorced widow benefit that you would be receiving if you were not receiving a social security benefit through your own work. (*See* "The Dual Entitlement Rule," page 57.) In other words, this formula assumes that your whole social security benefit is a divorced widow benefit, whether it actually is or not.

In figuring the amount of your social security benefit that will be subtracted, the finance center *will not* count:

- Your social security divorced widow benefit that results from your ex-husband's earnings outside of the military.

- The portion of your social security divorced widow benefit that is being suspended if you are working and earning more money than social security allows retired people to earn and still collect their full benefits. (You will need to get a statement from your local social security office to prove the amount of your benefits that is being suspended.)

This offset can result in a reduction of no more than 40 percent of your SBP annuity. For example, a $550 SBP annuity could be reduced to $330 if the maximum offset is applied.

Reserves and National Guard

Some of the rules for the SBP annuity, including the way that it is figured, are different for members of the Reserves and the National Guard. You should ask your lawyer what rules will apply in your situation.

Ways the SBP Annuity Can Be Provided to a Former Spouse

You can receive the SBP annuity through either a court order or your former husband's voluntary election.

Court Order

When you negotiate your divorce, you may be able to get a court order providing for your former husband to elect the Survivor Benefit Plan annuity for you. A "court order" can either mean that the court orders him to choose the SBP for you, or orders him to make a written agreement with you that he will choose the SBP.

Even if he elected the SBP while you were married, he still needs to "choose" the SBP by asking the finance center to change your beneficiary designation to "former spouse." The court order can be issued even if your husband is not yet eligible to retire. *But remember: You will not be protected unless he is eligible to retire or actually retired at the time of his death. (See page 132.) The court order must have been issued after November 13, 1986 (when the law changed) for you to be paid the SBP annuity.*

The same court order can give you a share of the retired pay during your ex-husband's lifetime as well as the SBP annuity after he dies. The court order remains in effect unless a later court order changes the first order and your ex-husband sends the finance center a copy of the new order.

Voluntary Election

You can also receive the SBP annuity through a written agreement that you and your ex-husband sign.

- *Written Agreement.* You and your ex-husband may agree in writing that he will provide you the SBP. The agreement can be changed only if both you and your ex-husband sign another agreement to that effect.

- *Court-Approved Agreement.* If you and your ex-husband have a written agreement as described above, and that agreement is "incorporated in," "ratified by," or "approved by" a court order, your rights are better protected. Your ex-husband may then change his election only by getting a court to issue an order modifying the first court-approved agreement.

Enforcing Your Rights

Just getting a court order or written agreement providing that you are to receive the SBP annuity isn't enough. Your ex-husband must actually make an "election" for you. This means he must send the finance center a written statement, also signed by you, that notifies the finance center that he is making an election, and saying whether the choice is being made according to a court order or a written agreement. The finance center must receive the notice within *one year* after the date of your divorce.

Note: What if your ex-husband doesn't send the notice of election on time? You can protect yourself if you send the *court order* or *court-approved* written agreement that gives you the SBP annuity to the finance center. (*See* "Where to Send..." page 146.) Include a cover letter to the finance center that says you want to make a "deemed" election for the SBP. The finance center must receive your documents within one year after the date of the court order.

IMPORTANT: Unless you or your ex-husband makes an election within the time limits, you will not receive the SBP annuity no matter what your court order says.

Can Your Ex-husband Change the Election?

Once the election is made, your ex-husband will not be allowed to change the election unless he remarries and wants to provide the SBP annuity for his new wife *and* follows the specific requirements for changing the court order or agreement, as discussed above.

Supplemental Survivor Benefit Available

When your husband becomes eligible to elect SBP coverage, he will also have the chance to sign up for an additional survivor benefit. The "Supplemental Survivor Benefit Plan" provides a survivor with an extra benefit equal to up to 20 percent of the retired pay to make up for the age-62 reduction in the basic SBP annuity.

This benefit can be elected for a current or former spouse, and requires an additional reduction in the husband's retired pay. It is voluntary on his part and cannot be ordered by a court. It can, however, be provided to a former spouse as part of a court-approved property settlement.

The supplemental benefit must be elected prior to retirement, with one exception. If your husband retired before 1992 when this option began, he would have had one year ending on March 31, 1993, to sign up. If he did so, then you may be able to include the benefit as part of your property settlement, along with the basic SBP.

Will Children's Benefits Affect Your SBP Annuity?

The Survivor Benefit Plan may also be used to provide survivor annuities for the member's dependent children, but this will not affect the amount of the ex-wife's SBP annuity. The retiree, however, must accept a greater reduction in his own benefit in order to provide the SBP annuity to a former wife *and* their child or children.

How Does Remarriage Affect Your SBP Annuity?

Your remarriage after you reach age 55 does not affect your SBP annuity. If you are eligible to receive more than one SBP annuity because you were married to more than one military member, you can receive the larger of the two benefits but not both at the some time.

You will lose your benefit if you remarry before age 55. If your ex-husband has remarried, his current wife may then be eligible to receive the SBP annuity. If no one is eligible for the SBP annuity and the retiree is still living, his future retired pay will no longer be reduced.

The SBP annuity, or your future right to it, is restored if your new marriage ends in divorce or annulment or if your new husband dies.

Your ex-husband's remarriage has no effect on your future right to the SBP annuity.

Will You Be Eligible for Other Monthly Benefits?

In addition to regular retired pay, there are several other types of monthly benefits paid by the military or the Department of Veterans Affairs that are not specifically covered by the USFSPA. For the most part, these benefits are not available to ex-wives. These include:

- *Disability Retirement Benefits*. Federal law provides that military disability retirement benefits may not be treated as marital property at divorce, except for that portion of the benefits that the retiree may receive because he became more disabled after retirement.

- *VA Disability Compensation*. A few courts have treated VA disability compensation as *marital property*. However, you cannot get direct payment of a marital property share of these benefits. It may be possible to have VA disability compensation treated as a source for support payments. The U.S. Supreme Court has ruled that an ex-husband could be required to pay court-ordered child support out of his VA disability compensation. This decision suggests that an ex-husband could also be required to pay spousal support or alimony to his former spouse from his VA disability payments.

- *DIC Payments.* Once you are divorced, you cannot be eligible for monthly Dependency and Indemnity Compensation (DIC) payments. The VA normally pays DIC payments to the widow of a military member or retiree who dies from a service-connected cause or who dies after being disabled from a service-connected cause. Just being separated from your husband could make you ineligible. DIC payments are not payable to a widow who has not lived continuously with her husband if the VA determines that the separation was "her fault."

- *VA Pension.* A divorced wife cannot share in a VA pension, either while her ex-husband is living or after his death. This monthly benefit is paid to war veterans and their surviving spouses who are disabled or over age 65 and whose income is below a certain amount. A separated spouse may also be ineligible: the widow of a veteran cannot receive a VA pension if she did not live continuously with her husband during her marriage and the VA determines that the separation was "her fault."

- *Pre-1972 Survivor's Plan.* Even if your husband signed up for a survivor benefit for you when he retired, you may not be able to get a survivor benefit after divorce if he retired before September 21, 1972, when the Survivor Benefit Plan (SBP) was first established. Someone who retired before that date could provide a survivor benefit only through an earlier survivors' plan, called the Retired Serviceman's Family Protection Plan (RSFPP). Only 15 percent of retirees signed up for this protection, partly because they had to take a fairly large reduction in their own benefits to pay for it. But if a retiree did sign up, this type of survivor benefit cannot be extended to a divorced wife, even if the retiree is willing to provide it.

However, pre-1972 retirees were given at least two chances after 1972 to choose a survivor benefit under the SBP, and many retirees did so. If your husband retired before 1972, you should find out as part of your divorce proceedings whether he elected the SBP for you at any time after his retirement.

- *Separation Pay.* To help "downsize" the military, many servicemembers are being encouraged to leave before becoming eligible for retirement. Instead of retired pay, members who leave early are being offered "separation pay," which may be a lump sum or equal payments over a number of years. Federal law does not say whether a divorce court may treat this benefit as marital property, and no direct payment is available. Congress is considering legislation, however, that would let separation pay be divided like retired pay and paid by the finance center to former spouses. If your husband is still on active duty with fewer than 20 years of service, ask your lawyer whether your property settlement agreement should mention these benefits.

Even if your decree mentions sharing in the retired pay only, you may be able to claim part of the separation pay on the grounds that the separation pay in effect replaces the member's retired pay. But you would probably have to go back to court to do this, and, if successful, collect from your ex-husband rather than the finance center.

If You Are Already Divorced

Getting a Share of the Retired Pay

If you were divorced before June 26, 1981, and you were not awarded a share of the retired pay, a 1990 federal law prohibits you from returning to court to claim a share of those benefits as marital property, unless the divorce court "reserved jurisdiction" over the issue of dividing the retired pay.

If you were divorced between June 25, 1981, and February 1, 1983, and you were not awarded a share of the retired pay, you may be able to get a share now. Although USFSPA officially went into effect on February 1, 1983, it has been interpreted as allowing a division of retired pay for former spouses divorced on or after June 26, 1981, the date of the U.S. Supreme Court's *McCarty* decision. As a result, a number of courts and state legislatures have allowed military ex-wives divorced between those dates to go back to court and get their original divorce decrees changed, awarding them a share of the retired pay the retiree receives during his life.

If you were divorced after January 31, 1983, and you were not awarded a share of the retired pay, your rights will depend on what your state divorce law says about going back to court after a divorce is final. (*See* "After the Divorce," page 41.)

Getting the SBP

If you are already divorced, a court cannot now award you a Survivor Benefit Plan annuity.

Government Re-employment

If a military retiree goes to work as a civilian for the federal government, part of his military retired pay may be suspended while he is working. This rule is more likely to affect retired officers than retired enlisted members. As long as your former husband is not receiving a portion of his retired pay, your share may be reduced or eliminated.

If your ex-husband works long enough to become eligible for a federal civilian pension, he will have the option of giving up his military retired pay permanently in order to receive a single, larger government pension that includes both his military and civilian service. This means that your pension rights would be determined under the federal civilian retirement rules rather than the military retirement rules. You will not be fully protected if your court order only provides you a share of military retired pay or the military SBP annuity.

If there is any chance that your former husband will go to work for the government after retirement, your lawyer may want to include in your court order a provision for a share of your ex-husband's future civilian pension, in case he chooses to waive his military retired pay. The Office of Personnel Management has a model paragraph that can be used in your court order for this purpose. (*See* reference, *A Handbook for Attorneys,* page 113 of this book.) Although you would already have sent your court order to the military finance center, you should also send a copy to OPM if and when your husband begins civilian employment. Your court order also might provide that your ex-husband himself pay you an amount equal to your share of the retired pay if his military benefits are stopped while he is working.

If you were expecting to receive the SBP and want to protect your survivor rights, then your court order should also provide for a survivor annuity from OPM. Otherwise you probably won't receive survivor benefits from either the military or OPM if your ex-husband remarries.

Getting Information

If you or your lawyer wants to make a rough estimate of your husband's benefits, there are several books on military retirement that have charts for figuring retired pay according to a retiree's rank and years of service. If you need more exact answers about what he receives, your lawyer can ask your husband to give the military finance center a written authorization allowing it to provide the information.

Also, the military finance centers will respond to "interrogatories" from your lawyer, that is, formal written questions related to your court case. (*See below* for addresses of the military finance centers.)

If your husband has already retired, you may be able to find out the amount of his retired pay and what deductions are being made by sending a letter to the finance center. Your letter should say that you are requesting this information under the Freedom of Information Act. Sometimes, a wife or former wife may be able to find out the amount of the retired pay by telephoning the finance center.

Where to Send Retired Pay Court Orders

Air Force, Marine Corps, Navy
DFAS Cleveland Center
Cleveland, OH 44199
(216) 522-5301

Army
DFAS Indianapolis Center
Indianapolis, IN 46249
(317) 542-2155

Coast Guard and NOAA
Topeka Center
444 S.E. Quincy St.
Topeka, KS 66683-3591
(913) 295-2657

U.S. Public Health Service
Compensation Branch
Rockville Center
Parklawn Bldg.
5600 Fishers Lane
Rockville, MD 20857
(301) 443-6132

IMPORTANT: Addresses and telephone numbers of the finance centers change frequently. Don't wait until the last minute to get information you may need for your divorce. Be sure you have the current address before mailing any important information to the finance center. You are required to send your court order by certified mail. Always keep a copy of important documents.

CHAPTER 6

THE RAILROAD RETIREMENT SYSTEM

THE RAILROAD RETIREMENT SYSTEM

How the Railroad Retirement System Works

Most workers included under the railroad retirement system are employees of interstate railroads, railroad associations, and railroad labor unions. However, not every employee of a railroad is covered. Also, some workers are covered by the railroad retirement system even though they are not employed in the railroad industry.

Railroad retirement benefits are paid for with contributions from employers, and with railroad retirement taxes deducted from employees' paychecks. The railroad retirement system is administered and regulated by the Railroad Retirement Board, a federal agency.

An employee must have at least 10 years of service under the railroad retirement system to be eligible to collect a railroad pension. (If your ex-husband had railroad "credits," but not enough to be eligible for a railroad benefit, his credits will be transferred to the Social Security Administration for payment of a social security benefit.) An employee with fewer than 30 years of service may collect a "full" (unreduced) pension at age 65 or a reduced pension at age 62. An employee with at least 30 years of service may collect a full pension at age 62, or a reduced pension at age 60. A worker who becomes disabled can collect a disability pension with as few as 10 years of service.

A monthly pension that the retiree can collect during his lifetime is called a *"railroad annuity"* and consists of several parts. A retiree usually receives what are called "Tier 1" and "Tier 2" benefits. If he meets additional requirements, he may also receive a Vested Dual Benefit *or* a Supplemental Annuity, but not both.

Tier 1 Annuity

The "first tier" annuity is figured like a social security benefit, and is based on the retiree's lifetime earnings, whether from railroad employment or other, non-railroad employment under social security. (*See* Chapter 1, Social Security, page 51.) Social security credits earned by the retiree are transferred to the Railroad Retirement Board to be included in a combined Tier 1 annuity paid by the Board. Tier 1 annuities, including those paid to family members, receive the same cost of living increases as social security benefits.

Tier 2 Benefit

The "second tier" benefit is based on railroad retirement credits only, and is comparable to a company pension. Tier 2 benefits receive one-third the cost of living increase added to Tier 1 annuities.

Vested Dual Benefit

A worker may be entitled to a "vested dual benefit" if he had enough service before 1975 to qualify separately for both railroad and social security benefits, and if he met certain other requirements. This benefit never receives a cost of living increase.

Supplemental Annuity

A worker may qualify for a "Supplemental Annuity" as early as age 60 if he has at least 30 years of railroad service. Or, he can collect the annuity at age 65 with at least 25 years of railroad service. There are also other requirements for this benefit. The most important is that the retiree have a "current connection" with the railroad industry. This usually means that the retiree has worked for a railroad employer for at least 12 of the last 30 months (2 1/2 years) just before becoming entitled to a railroad annuity. This benefit never receives a cost of living increase.

Note: Some retirees may also qualify for separate company pensions based on their work for a railroad-connected employer. (*See* Chapter 2, "Private Pensions.")

Railroad Benefits for Divorced Wives

Various benefits are available to divorced wives. You can get some benefits just by applying for them; others must be awarded by a court.

In 1979, the United States Supreme Court ruled, in the case of *Hisquierdo* v. *Hisquierdo,* that railroad retirement benefits could *not* be divided at divorce. However, Congress later (in 1981 and 1983) passed legislation partly overruling that decision and making it possible for divorced spouses to qualify for benefits.

Note: The Railroad Retirement System often uses the word "wife" to refer to a woman whose husband is living, and "widow" or "mother" to refer to someone whose husband has died.

Your Rights While Your Ex-husband Is Living

Tier 1 Annuity

If you are divorced, you may be able to qualify for a Tier 1 divorced wife annuity when you reach age 62. Your annuity is a separate amount that does not reduce your ex-husband's annuity, and it is the same amount you would have received had your ex-husband's earnings all been under social security. Your basic benefit is equal to 50 percent of the unreduced Tier 1 annuity your ex-husband would receive if he started collecting at age 65, even if he chooses a reduced benefit at an earlier age. The amount of your annuity will be permanently reduced if *you* start collecting before you are 65.*

---

* If you were born before 1938, the maximum reduction is 25 percent. If you were born after 1937, the maximum reduction may be as much as 35 percent, depending on the year you were born.

Note: There are instances in which a retired worker's Tier 1 annuity is somewhat larger than his social security benefit would be if all his earnings had been under social security. However, the Tier 1 annuity for a divorced spouse is never more than her equivalent social security benefit.

Tier 1 annuities are available to divorced wives who apply after October 1, 1981. The eligibility rules for the Tier 1 annuity are similar to those for social security: the major difference is that you cannot collect a Tier 1 annuity until your ex-husband starts collecting his annuity. (*See* Chapter 1, "Social Security," page 49.) You become automatically entitled to the Tier 1 annuity by making an application through the Railroad Retirement Board and meeting the following requirements:

- You and your ex-husband must both be at least 62 years old.

- The marriage must have lasted at least 10 consecutive years, regardless of whether your ex-husband's railroad service occurred during that period.

- You must not have remarried since your divorce.

- Your ex-husband must have begun collecting his own railroad retirement or disability annuity. (The disability must satisfy the definition of "total disability" used for social security benefits.)

You get the Tier 1 annuity automatically if you qualify. A court cannot award or deny you the Tier 1 divorced wife annuity, and cannot in any other way treat this benefit as marital property.

The divorced wife annuity can be paid until you or your ex-husband dies. After his death, you will become eligible for a survivor annuity. (*See* "Your Rights After Your Ex-husband Dies," page 155.)

Other events, such as remarriage or work after retirement, may also stop your benefits. (*See* page 159.)

During the employee's lifetime, the Railroad Retirement Board will not pay a disability annuity to a divorced wife who is or becomes disabled. However, after the employee's death, a disabled divorced wife may become eligible for a disabled divorced *widow* annuity as early as age 50. (*See* page 156.)

Tier 2 and Other Benefits

The Tier 2 Benefit, Vested Dual Benefit, and Supplemental Annuity *may* be treated as marital property at divorce and a court may award you a share to be paid directly by the Railroad Retirement Board. Your share will be taken out of your former husband's benefits and reduce the amount he receives. A divorced wife does not automatically qualify for a share of the retiree's Tier 2 and other benefits, but must obtain her share through a court order.

The Railroad Retirement Board says that you cannot be awarded a share of the Tier 2 Benefit, Vested Dual Benefit, and Supplemental Annuity as alimony or support; it can only be awarded as marital property. But your ex-husband's benefits may be garnished to pay the alimony or support that he owes you. (*See* "Garnishment," page 40.)

Your Rights After Your Ex-husband Dies

Tier 1 Annuity

After your ex-husband dies, you may be eligible for one of three survivor benefits if your ex-husband had enough service under the railroad retirement system to qualify for his own Tier 1 annuity, whether or not he ever collected one. (*See* page 152.)

Note: If your ex-husband did not have a "current connection," (*See* page 152), your survivor annuity will be paid by the Social Security Administration rather than the Railroad Retirement Board. Your social security survivor annuity will still be equal to the railroad Tier 1 survivor annuity.

Survivor Benefits Available to Divorced Spouses

A *divorced widow annuity* is payable if you are at least age 60 when you apply and you were married 10 years or more.

A *disabled divorced widow annuity* is payable if you are at least age 50 and severely disabled and you were married 10 years or more.

A *surviving divorced mother annuity* is payable as long as you have in your care the worker's child who is under 16 or disabled, and the child is collecting an annuity from the Railroad Retirement Board. Your annuity is payable regardless of the length of your marriage or how young you are.

Both the divorced widow annuity and the disabled divorced widow annuity are equal to 100 percent of the Tier 1 annuity your former husband was receiving (or was eligible to receive). Both annuities will be permanently reduced if you start collecting benefits before age 65. The maximum reduction of 28 1/2 percent applies to each annuity if you start collecting at age 60 or earlier.

The surviving divorced mother annuity is equal to 75 percent of your ex-husband's age-65 annuity. Unlike the other two survivor benefits, your surviving divorced mother annuity is not reduced if you are under 65.

You may not be remarried when you apply for any of these benefits. Remarrying *after* you start collecting may affect your benefit. (*See* "Remarriage," page 159.)

Note: If you think you may be eligible for a Tier 1 annuity, you should apply even if you don't know where your ex-husband is, whether or not he has retired or died, or what his social security number is. The Railroad Retirement Board can usually help you obtain necessary information.

Tier 2 and Other Benefits

Although you may be awarded a share of the retiree's Tier 2 and other benefits while he is living, *these benefits cannot be paid after he dies. The Railroad Retirement Board will not honor a court order awarding you a survivor annuity from these benefits.* Your ex-husband also cannot voluntarily provide you a survivor annuity from these benefits.

Note: Since the Tier 2 Benefit, Vested Dual Benefit, and Supplemental Annuity cannot be paid after the ex-husband dies, a railroad survivor annuity for a *divorced* widow is less than for a *married* widow because it is based on the ex-husband's Tier 1 annuity *only*.

Understanding Your Court Order

What Is a "Court Order"?

Under the Railroad Retirement System, the term "court order" can mean a final decree of divorce or annulment, a court-approved legal separation agreement, a court-approved property settlement, or a modification of any of the above. The court order must say that the Railroad Retirement Board (rather than your ex-husband) is to pay you a share of the railroad benefits. The order must specify the amount to be paid, either as a dollar amount, fraction, or percentage.

Remember, there is no requirement in the railroad retirement system that the Tier 2 Benefit, Vested Dual Benefit, and Supplemental Annuity *must* be divided at divorce. The law only says that a state divorce court *may* divide the benefits.

Note: The law allowing for a division of the Tier 2 and other benefits as marital property applies to orders issued on or after September 1, 1983. A court order issued before that date, including one that is later modified, may be accepted by the Railroad Retirement Board, assuming the court order meets all other requirements and is received after September 1, 1983.

How Much Can You Get?

A court may award you part or all of the *"net"* benefits that are payable to your ex-husband. The net benefits are the retiree's Tier 2 Benefit, Vested Dual Benefit, and Supplemental Annuity, minus any amounts he owes to the United States government, such as payments for Medicare premiums or repayments of benefits mistakenly paid to him. If it is specified in the court order, you can also share in any cost of living increases your ex-husband receives from the Tier 2 benefit. (Remember, the other two benefits don't receive cost of living increases.)

Note: The Railroad Retirement Board will not accept a court order that awards you a share of your ex-husband's "contributions," that is, the money he paid into the railroad retirement system. You can only get a share of your ex-husband's "benefits," the money that is paid out to him.

How Is Your Share Paid?

You can receive a share of the monthly benefits the retiree receives as they are paid to him. The Board does not pay retirement benefits as a lump sum to either retirees or former wives.

When Do Payments Start and Stop?

The court order must specify when payments are to start and stop. Federal law does not require that you be a certain age before payments can start, but they cannot start before your ex-husband's payments begin.

You cannot receive payments for months in which your ex-husband is not being paid retirement benefits because he is working. (*See* page 160.)

Your payments will stop when you die, when your ex-husband dies, or at any earlier point specified in the court order. (For example, the court order might say that your payments stop after a certain number of years.)

See "What To Do With Your Court Order," page 161.

Factors That Can Affect Your Benefits

Remarriage

If you remarry, your benefits may be affected.

- *Tier 1 Divorced Wife Annuity.* Your annuity stops if you remarry at any age, but it can be restored if your new marriage ends.

- *Tier 1 Divorced Widow Annuity.* You cannot collect this annuity if you remarry before age 60 unless your new marriage ends through the death of your husband, divorce, or annulment. Remarriage after age 60 will not affect your benefit.

- *Tier 1 Disabled Divorced Widow Annuity.* You won't be able to collect this annuity if you remarry before you are age 50 and become disabled. You can become eligible for the annuity if your new marriage ends through the death of your husband, divorce, or annulment. Remarriage after you are age 50 and become disabled will not affect your benefit.

- *Tier 1 Surviving Divorced Mother Annuity.* The annuity stops if you remarry at any age, unless your new husband receives social security or railroad benefits. (*But see* "Offsets of Other Benefits," page 161.) Your annuity can be restored if your new marriage ends and you still have an eligible child in your care. Even if the surviving divorced mother annuity stops, you may become eligible for a divorced *widow* annuity once you meet the age and other requirements.

- *Tier 2 and Other Benefits.* Your court-ordered share of the Tier 2 Benefit, Vested Dual Benefit, and Supplemental Annuity will not be affected by your remarriage unless your court order says so.

If your former husband remarries, none of the railroad benefits you receive as a divorced spouse will be affected. The fact that his wife or another ex-wife collects a spouse benefit does not affect your benefit, except that there is a maximum monthly amount of Tier 1 benefits payable based on one retiree's earnings. This maximum varies according to the amount of the retiree's railroad earnings. If the total amount of benefits payable to family members (including you) exceeds this maximum, then your Tier 1 annuity and the Tier 1 annuities of the other family members will be reduced by the same proportion.

Ask the nearest Railroad Retirement Board office for more information on how the "family maximum" rule may affect your benefit.

Work After Retirement

You may lose part of your Tier 1 benefit if you or your ex-husband goes back to work after retirement.

If you receive a Tier 1 divorced *wife* annuity, your annuity is not payable for any month that you work after retirement if you work for a railroad employer or for your last employer before retirement (known as the "last person service" rule). Your annuity will stop for the months that you work regardless of how little money you earn. Survivor benefits are not affected by these restrictions.

If you are under age 70, your Tier 1 annuity may be reduced if you have earnings over a certain amount within a calendar year, regardless of where you work. You may lose part or all of your Tier 1 annuity (including the survivor annuity) in that year. Under the "earnings test," the exact amount you can earn before you start losing benefits increases each year and varies according to your age. A different earnings test applies to *disabled* widows.

If your ex-husband goes back to work after retirement and if his annuity is not payable during the time he is working, *your* annuity will also stop in any month that his does.

"Offsets" of Other Benefits

You may lose all or part of your Tier 1 divorced spouse annuity if you have worked and earned your own railroad retirement Tier 1 annuity, a social security benefit, or a federal, state, or local government pension. Any of these benefits may be counted against your railroad spouse annuity.

Your Tier 1 divorced spouse annuity may also be reduced if you are entitled to another railroad Tier 1 spouse annuity or a social security spouse benefit. This could happen if you had been married to another husband who worked for the railroad or under social security.

If you receive or expect to receive any of the benefits mentioned above, you should ask the nearest Railroad Retirement Board office about what effect your other benefit(s) will have on your railroad divorced spouse annuity.

What to Do With Your Court Order

Send a recent official copy of your court order by certified mail to:

Deputy General Counsel
Railroad Retirement Board
844 Rush Street
Chicago, IL 60611

Along with the order, include a letter with the following information:

- Your former husband's full name and current address
- His social security number or railroad retirement claim number
- His date of birth
- Your full name and current address
- Your social security number

What to Do With Your Court Order (cont.)

You must also include a statement that you will notify the Board if an event occurs that would stop your payments. For example, if the court order says that your share is to stop when you remarry, it is up to you to notify the Board of your remarriage and return any checks incorrectly paid to you after that date.

When the Board gets your court order, it will make sure the order meets all the requirements. If it does, the Board will then notify you and your ex-husband that the order "qualifies" and tell you the amount of the benefit you will be getting. If the order doesn't qualify, the Board will tell you why it doesn't. Whether you can get the court order changed depends on your state divorce law.

If your former husband hasn't yet retired, the Board will tell you whether the order qualifies, and then keep the order until he applies for retirement. When he applies for benefits, the Board will notify you that your checks are starting, so it is important for you to let the Board know if your address changes.

Once it is time for your share to start being paid, the Board will tell you what documents it needs from you in order to start paying your Tier 2 and other benefits. While it is waiting to get those documents, the Board will withhold your share from your ex-husband's Tier 2 and other benefits for up to three months. It will pay you the withheld amount once it receives your documents.

If the Board doesn't hear from you within the three months, the withheld benefits will be paid to your ex-husband. If, after that, the Board then gets a response from you, it will be able to pay you only your share of the future benefits paid to your ex-husband from that point on, but not the money already withheld.

Getting Information

Usually a wife needs the written permission of the employee or retiree in order to get information about his benefits. But once either spouse has filed for divorce or legal separation, you or your lawyer can write to request information from the Railroad Retirement Board.

The Board will provide information such as the amount of monthly benefits your husband is getting, or the estimated amount he would be entitled to if he were now at retirement age. The Board will not figure the lump sum value of his benefits or predict what his benefits might be based on future earnings. You can make your request through the Board at the Chicago address on page 161 or through a local Railroad Retirement Board office (*See* U.S. Government listings in your telephone book). No court order is necessary for getting information.

If you have questions about the Railroad Retirement Board's requirements for sharing in benefits through a court order, you can telephone the Board at (312) 751-4936.

CHAPTER 7

THE FOREIGN SERVICE
RETIREMENT SYSTEM

THE FOREIGN SERVICE RETIREMENT SYSTEM

How the Foreign Service Retirement System Works

The Foreign Service Retirement and Disability System (FSRDS) covers members of the Foreign Service who were hired before 1984.* This retirement system is run by the U.S. Department of State.

Foreign Service employees make up a small percentage of the employees in the State Department. Some members of the Foreign Service work for one of several other small agencies, such as the Agency for International Development and the United States Information Agency. Most employees in the State Department who are not in the Foreign Service are covered by the Civil Service Retirement System or the Federal Employees Retirement System.

An employee is *not* covered by social security while he is working under FSRDS.

An employee who works at least five years under FSRDS will be eligible for a lifetime monthly benefit, called an *"annuity,"* at retirement age, usually age 60. He may collect an annuity at an earlier retirement age if he has at least 20 years of service and works up to age 50. An employee who leaves government service before retirement age must wait until age 60 to collect an annuity. A disabled employee with at least five years of service may start collecting a disability retirement annuity at any age. An employee covered by the Foreign Service Retirement and Disability System is called a *"participant."*

---

* Foreign Service employees hired in 1984 or after are covered by the Foreign Service Pension System (FSPS) which is not discussed in this handbook. Employees already covered by FSRDS were given a short time to transfer to the new system if they chose to do so.

Both the employee and the government pay into FSRDS. However, the monthly annuity a retiree receives is based on the number of years he worked and his average earnings, not on how much money was paid in. An employee who leaves the government before retirement age may choose to withdraw his own contributions and give up the right to collect an annuity later. No interest is paid on the refunded contributions if the employee worked five years or more.

Foreign Service annuities are more generous than most other federal government annuities. Otherwise, rules for workers under FSRDS are very similar to those under the federal Civil Service Retirement System. For example, military service and any federal civilian service (such as work for another federal agency) can be counted toward a Foreign Service annuity. The annuities paid to retirees and their survivors generally receive cost of living increases each year.

Foreign Service Benefits for Divorced Wives

An important difference between the Foreign Service Retirement and Disability System and other federal employee retirement systems is that FSRDS provides a "fall-back" share of benefits to certain former wives, both while the employee is living and after he dies. The fall-back provisions were created by the Foreign Service Act of 1980 to help spouses who were not awarded a share of the annuity as part of the divorce. The 1980 law also provides other ways that former spouses may receive benefits.*

---

* If your former husband receives a *disability* annuity, your lawyer should know about the special laws and regulations for disability annuities that may affect how much and when you may be paid your share of benefits.

Your Rights While Your Ex-husband Is Living

A divorced wife may receive a portion of the Foreign Service annuity through the fall-back provisions of the law, through a court order, or through a "spousal agreement." Her share is called a *"former spouse pension,"* although it is taken out of the retiree's *annuity*, and may be paid directly to her by the State Department.

Instead of awarding you a former spouse pension, a court is permitted to treat the Foreign Service annuity as marital property, and award you other marital assets equal in value to what would have been your share of the annuity.

Fall-back Share

You may be entitled to a fall-back (or statutory) share of the annuity if you meet *all* of the following requirements.

- You must have been divorced after February 14, 1981.

- Your ex-husband must have stopped working under the Foreign Service after February 14, 1981, or started collecting a Foreign Service annuity after that date.

- You and your ex-husband must have been married for at least 10 years of his *"creditable service,"* that is, government service that is counted toward his Foreign Service annuity. In at least five of those years he must have been working in the Foreign Service.

- You must not have remarried before age 55.

This is a fall-back benefit in the sense that you receive it only if there isn't a court order or a "spousal agreement" that says who gets the annuity.

169

Court Order or Spousal Agreement

Most divorced Foreign Service wives receive a share of a retirement annuity through a *qualified court order* or a *spousal agreement*, instead of the fall-back provision. To get a share through a court order or a spousal agreement, you need to have been married at least nine months.

A *"qualified court order"* can be a court decree of divorce or any court-approved property settlement having to do with your divorce. To be "qualified," the court order must meet the following requirements:

- The order was issued by a court of a state or a U.S. territory, or U.S. Indian court.

- It provides that payments be made to a former spouse out of the employee's Foreign Service retirement benefits or survivor benefits.

- It provides the amount to be paid, or a formula for payment that the State Department can easily calculate.

- It was issued within 24 months after your final divorce decree.

Since September 15, 1978, former spouses have been allowed by law to receive a share of a Foreign Service annuity through a court order. (*Survivor* annuities could not be provided to former spouses until a later date.)

A *"spousal agreement"* is a legal written agreement between the employee and his wife or former wife. Unlike a *court order*, it does not have to be issued or approved by a court; it only needs to be notarized or "authenticated" by a court. The agreement must provide the amount to be paid, or a formula for payment that the State Department can easily calculate.

If your spousal agreement is signed after your ex-husband has remarried, his new wife must also sign the agreement. The agreement must be filed with the State Department. (*See* "What To Do With Your Court Documents," page 182.) Before the agreement is signed and mailed, your lawyer may want to check with the State Department to make sure the proposed agreement will be accepted as written.

How Much Can You Get?

Fall-back Share

Your fall-back share may be as much as 50 percent of your former husband's annuity if you were married during all his years of creditable government service, but less than 50 percent (a "pro rata" share) if you were married for only some of his government service. Your share is figured this way:

■ Example 1: Married during all years of service

Lillian was married to Edward during all his years of creditable government service. Edward has earned a Foreign Service annuity of $1000 a month after 20 years.

50%	x	Edward's monthly annuity	=	Lillian's former spouse pension

50%	x	$1000*	=	$500

Lillian's former spouse pension would be $500 a month. Her benefit will increase each year as Edward's benefit is increased with the cost of living.

---

* This is the amount of his annuity *after* the reduction for Lillian's widow's pension. (*See* "Amount of retiree's annuity," page 172.)

■ Example 2: Married during only part of creditable service

Let's say Lillian was married to Edward for 10 years, half his years of creditable service. In this case, she receives a pro rata share, that is, 50 percent of that portion of the annuity *earned during their marriage.*

$$50\% \times \left\{ \frac{\text{Number of years married during creditable service}}{\text{Total number of years of creditable service}} \times \text{Edward's monthly annuity} \right\} = \text{Lillian's former spouse pension}$$

$$50\% \times \left\{ \frac{10}{20} \times \$2000 \right\} = \text{Lillian's former spouse pension}$$

$$50\% \times \$500 = \$250$$

Lillian's former spouse pension will be $250 a month when Edward starts collecting his annuity.

Creditable service. For purposes of figuring the amount of the former wife's share, *creditable service* in the above example does not include certain "extra" years of service that may be credited when an employee becomes disabled or dies before retirement age.

Amount of retiree's annuity. The fall-back provision formula uses the retiree's whole annuity, *minus* the reduction that would be required if the retiree provides a survivor annuity to that same former wife. (*See* page 181.) No other deductions are taken into account.

172

Court Order or Spousal Agreement

If your court order or spousal agreement provides for it, the State Department will pay directly to you as much as 100 percent of the retiree's *"net"* annuity. The net annuity is what is left of the annuity after the following deductions:

- Debts the retiree owes the government

- Health and life insurance premiums

- The retiree's repayment of any government benefits mistakenly paid to him

- Federal income taxes (up to certain limits)

- Annuity reduction taken to provide a survivor annuity

A court order or a spousal agreement can be used to provide you with an amount more or less than you would receive under the fall-back provision, or it can say that you will receive *no* benefits. (For example, you might agree to accept other property rather than a share of the annuity.) However, many court orders and spousal agreements provide the former wife with the same, or almost the same, amount of benefits that would be payable under the fall-back sharing provisions.

IMPORTANT: *Don't assume that the court will automatically give you a share of benefits equal to the pro rata share, especially if your husband opposes splitting the pension with you. (See page 171.) Your lawyer will still need to persuade the court that you are entitled to this share under state divorce law.*

Note: If a court *did* award you 100 percent of the retiree's whole annuity, you would have to collect the amount over the net annuity directly from the retiree rather than from the State Department.

When Do Payments Start?

Fall-back Share

Once the State Department decides that your divorce decree is valid, payments will start from the first month in which your divorce is final, or the month in which your former husband starts receiving his annuity, whichever is later. You can receive payments from that date even if the State Department doesn't receive notice of your decree until a later date. In other words, the State Department will make retroactive payments.

Court Order or Spousal Agreement

Payment can start from the date that the State Department approves your court order or spousal agreement, or the date when your former husband starts collecting his annuity, whichever is later. The court order can specifically provide that your payments are to be made retroactively, that is, payable from the date of divorce. However, if you use a spousal agreement, you cannot ask for retroactive payments.

When Do Payments Stop?

Death or remarriage can stop your former spouse pension. The following rules apply whether you are collecting your benefit through the fall-back provisions, a court order, or a spousal agreement.

Death

If the retiree dies before you, your share of his annuity stops. However, a survivor annuity may then be payable to you. (*See* page 178.)

If you die before the retiree, your payments stop, and from that point the retiree will collect his full annuity.

Remarriage

If you remarry before age 55, your former spouse pension stops permanently, even if your new marriage later ends. *You can avoid losing benefits, however, if your spousal agreement or court order expressly provides that your payments are to continue even if you remarry.* In any case, remarriage at age 55 or later has no effect on your benefits. *If your ex-husband remarries*, your payments are not affected.

Your Rights After Your Ex-husband Dies

Once your ex-husband dies, you cannot receive a *former spouse pension*. You may, however, be entitled to a survivor annuity if your ex-husband retired and died after February 14, 1981, when the Foreign Service Act of 1980 went into effect. This benefit, called a *former spouse survivor annuity*, may be provided to a divorced wife in one of three ways: through the fall-back provisions, a court order, or a spousal agreement.

The former spouse survivor annuity is really the same benefit as a *current* spouse survivor annuity, the benefit you would have received had you remained married, but the rules for getting a former spouse survivor annuity are more complicated.

Usually, the State Department will only pay out an amount equal to one survivor annuity, whether it is paid all to the worker's current wife or all to the former wife, or divided between the two wives.

The *retiree's* annuity is reduced if the former wife or current wife is entitled to a survivor annuity. (*See* page 182.) Survivor annuities, like retired employee annuities, usually get cost of living increases each year.

The Foreign Service Retirement and Disability System survivor annuity is not affected by any annuity you may be receiving through your own work.

Death Before Retirement

If a Foreign Service member dies while still employed, his divorced wife may be eligible for a survivor annuity if a court order or a spousal agreement provides it, or through the fall-back provisions if her ex-husband worked at least five years under Foreign Service. There is no cost to the employee to protect a former wife in case of his death while he is still employed.

If a Foreign Service member dies after leaving federal employment but before starting to collect an annuity at retirement age, no annuity is payable to any survivor. Your ex-husband's death during this period means that you lose the right to a future share of his annuity as well as your survivor annuity.

The State Department will, however, pay to a "beneficiary" a lump sum refund of the contributions, plus interest, that the former husband paid into the FSRDS. A court order or a spousal agreement can also provide you all or a part of the lump sum. Under the fall-back sharing provision, you can claim 50 percent of the lump sum, or a pro rata share if you were married for less than the entire period of his creditable service.

Death After Retirement

If a Foreign Service member dies after starting to collect his annuity, a survivor annuity may be payable to his ex-wife. You can receive a survivor annuity through a court order or a spousal agreement or through the fall-back provisions.

Your Written Consent Needed to Give Up Survivor Annuity

Until 1981, a retiree alone had the choice whether to provide a survivor annuity or not. But now the law says that a married Foreign Service member who starts collecting his annuity after February 15, 1981, and who wants to provide less than the maximum survivor annuity or none at all, must get his wife's written consent. He doesn't have to get his wife's written consent if he can show that she can't be located.

Whether you are in the middle of divorce negotiations or you only suspect that a divorce may be in your future, think carefully before giving up (or "waiving") your survivor annuity. Once your husband has started collecting his annuity and you become divorced, you cannot become eligible again for survivor benefits you signed away.

Don't sign away your right to a survivor annuity in exchange for your husband's promise to give you his government life insurance (known as Federal Employees Government Life Insurance, or FEGLI). No matter what agreement you have with him — even if it's part of your court-approved property settlement — your husband has the right under federal law to name *anyone* as his FEGLI beneficiary, and he may remove you as beneficiary (and name someone else) at any time, even after you are divorced.

Ways To Provide a Survivor Annuity for a Former Wife

Fall-back Share

You may be entitled to a fall-back survivor annuity if you meet the requirements described on page 169 ("Fall-back Share"). Your ex-husband must have been working for the Foreign Service after February 14, 1981. You would receive this benefit only if you didn't have a valid court order or spousal agreement that says who gets the survivor annuity. You can receive this benefit whether your ex-husband dies while he is working for the government or after he starts collecting his annuity (but not if he dies after leaving the government and before retirement).

Court Order or Spousal Agreement

You may receive a former spouse survivor annuity through a qualified court order or a spousal agreement. The requirements for these are described on page 170 ("Court Order or Spousal Agreement"). A court order or a spousal agreement can be used to give you survivor protection whether your former husband dies while he is working for the government or after he starts collecting his annuity (but not if he dies after leaving the government and before retirement).

How Much can You Get?

Fall-back Share

The fall-back survivor annuity may be equal to as much as 55 percent of your former husband's entire annuity, but will be less than that (that is, a "pro rata" share) if you were married for only some of his creditable government service. Your survivor annuity is figured as if your ex-husband were receiving a *full* annuity with no reductions. The calculation of your benefit does not take into account any survivor annuity reduction that may be required in your ex-husband's annuity. It also does not take into account the share of his annuity — the former spouse pension — that is paid to you during his lifetime.

Your benefit is figured this way:

■ Example 1: Married during all creditable government service

Carol was married to Leonard for 20 years, all his creditable government service. Leonard has earned a Foreign Service annuity of $2000 a month.

55% x Leonard's monthly annuity = Carol's survivor annuity

55% x $2000*   = $1100

Carol's former spouse survivor annuity will be $1100 a month.

■ Example 2: Married for only part of creditable service

Let's say Carol was married to Leonard during only part of his government service, for 10 years. In this case, she receives a pro rata share, that is, 55 percent of that portion of the annuity *earned during their marriage.*

$$55\% \times \left\{ \frac{\text{Number of years married during creditable service}}{\text{Total number of years of creditable service}} \times \text{Leonard's monthly annuity} \right\} = \text{Carol's survivor annuity}$$

$$55\% \times \left\{ \frac{10}{20} \times \$2000^* \right\} = \text{Carol's survivor annuity}$$

$$55\% \times \$1000 = \$550$$

Carol's former spouse survivor annuity will be $550 a month.

* Leonard will receive less than $2000 a month since he must accept a reduction to provide the survivor annuity. (*See* "Amount of retiree's annuity," page 180.)

Creditable service. For the purpose of figuring the amount of the former spouse survivor annuity, creditable service does not include certain "extra" years of service that may be credited when an employee becomes disabled or dies before retirement age.

Amount of retiree's annuity. The fall-back sharing formula uses the entire amount of the retiree's annuity. If he dies while still working, his annuity amount is based on the number of years of service he had when he died.

The benefit your ex-husband receives at retirement will be reduced if he is providing you a survivor annuity. The reduction is equal to 2 1/2 percent of the first $300 a month (or $7.50) of his annuity, plus 10 percent of the rest of his annuity.

For example, the reduction in Leonard's annuity of $2000 a month would be figured this way:

$2000 − [(2 1/2 % of $300) + (10% of $1700)] = Leonard's reduced annuity

$2000 − [$7.50 + $170] = Leonard's reduced annuity

$2000 − [$177.50] = $1822.50

Leonard's benefit after the survivor annuity reduction would be $1822.50 a month.

If Carol is to receive only half the maximum survivor annuity, then the reduction in Leonard's annuity will be based on only half his benefit, or $1000. The reduction amount is then subtracted from his full annuity, or $2000.

$2000 − [(2 1/2 % of $300) + (10% of $700)] = Leonard's reduced annuity

$2000 − [$7.50 + $70] = Leonard's reduced annuity

$2000 − [$77.50] = $1922.50

Leonard will receive a benefit of $1922.50 after the reduction is applied. Carol's benefit will be 55 percent of $1000, or $550.

Court Order or Spousal Agreement

Your court order or spousal agreement can provide you an amount up to the maximum survivor annuity of 55 percent of your ex-husband's entire annuity (regardless of the length of your marriage), or it can say that you receive *no* survivor annuity. (This would be most likely to happen if you had agreed to accept some other property instead of the survivor annuity.)

IMPORTANT: Whether you are to receive a survivor annuity through the fall-back provision, a court order, or a spousal agreement, your benefit can never be more than the benefit you would have received if you had remained married. This means that if you signed away part or all of the survivor annuity while you were married, you cannot become entitled *after* divorce to benefits you have already signed away.

When Do Payments Start?

Whether you are to collect a survivor annuity under the fall-back sharing provisions, a court order, or a spousal agreement, payments start immediately following your ex-husband's death.

When Do Payments Stop?

Whether you are to collect a survivor annuity under the fall-back provisions, a court order, or a spousal agreement, your death or remarriage can stop your former spouse survivor annuity.

When you die, your right to the survivor annuity stops. You cannot choose someone else to receive your survivor annuity after your death. However, if you die after the survivor annuity has begun, but before an amount equal to your ex-husband's own contributions has been paid out, the rest of his contributions plus interest will be paid to the person he chose as his "beneficiary" for this purpose.

If you remarry before age 55, your right to benefits stops. But you can be eligible again to collect benefits if your new marriage ends in divorce, annulment, or your new husband's death. Remarriage at age 55 or later has no effect on your benefits.

If your former husband remarries, your future payments will not be affected.

If you die or remarry before age 55 while your ex-husband is still living, he can resume collecting his unreduced annuity. If he has remarried, he may choose to continue the reduction in his annuity to pay for a survivor annuity for his new wife.

What to Do With Your Court Documents

In order to collect your former spouse pension and survivor annuity, you or your lawyer will need to send certain documents and information to the State Department. If you are claiming the fall-back share, then you only need to show the Department proof that you have a valid divorce and meet the length-of-marriage requirement. But if you are claiming benefits under a court order or a spousal agreement, then the State Department must also review the order or agreement to see whether it is qualified. These requirements are explained in more detail below.

What to Send to the State Department

Fall-back Share

If your ex-husband notified the State Department of your divorce, the Department will contact you. If the Department has not done this, you should send it a letter in which you request payment. Be sure you also include:

- Your full name, address, and date of birth.
- Your ex-husband's full name and address.

- The dates of your marriage and divorce.

- A copy of your divorce decree, certified by the court clerk.

Court Order

To receive payment as provided in your court order, you need to send to the State Department a copy of the order and a completed application form. You can request an application form from the Department by mail, telephone, or in person. The application form asks for information such as:

- Your full name, address, date of birth, and current marital status.

- Your ex-husband's full name and date of birth.

- Dates of your marriage and divorce.

- A statement that the court order has not been "amended, superseded, or set aside" (in other words, changed).

- Your agreement to notify the Department if you remarry.

Also send a copy of your court order, certified by the court clerk, or enclose a statement that the order has already been sent.

Spousal Agreement

To receive payment as provided in your spousal agreement, you need to send that document to the State Department. The agreement should be sent as soon as possible and can be mailed even before you are divorced.

The State Department mailing address and telephone number are:

Chief, Retirement Division
Department of State
Attention: PER/ER/RET
Washington, DC 20520
(202) 647-9315

This is the address to use whether your former husband is still working or retired.

How the State Department Will Handle Your Request

Fall-back Share

Once the Department receives a copy of your decree, it will determine whether the decree is valid. Usually the Department will say the decree is valid unless either husband or wife has legally challenged the decree. If the decree is valid, the Department will then notify you and your ex-husband when payments will start.

Court Order

After the Department receives a copy of your court order or agreement, it will tell you if it needs additional information or documents in order to make a decision about whether the order is "qualified." If it determines that the order is not qualified, the Department will explain why it isn't.

Once the Department decides the order *is* qualified, it will send a notice of the decision to you and your ex-husband. The notice will say how much your payments will be, how they are to be figured, and when they will start. If your payments are to start immediately, the Department will withhold your share from your ex-husband's annuity for 30 days. If your ex-husband makes no objection to the order within the 30 days, the Department will start your payments.

If your ex-husband makes a legal objection to the order, the State Department will give him an additional 30 days to go to court. If he notifies the Department that he has started legal action within that period, the Department will continue to withhold your share until the issue is resolved. Once the matter is resolved, the Department will pay the withheld amount to the appropriate spouse.

Spousal Agreement

Once the Department receives your spousal agreement, it will tell you whether the agreement meets the requirements for spousal agreements that are set out in the law.

Special Former Spouse Benefits

A 1987 law provided automatic retirement and survivor annuities to certain Foreign Service ex-spouses. The main eligibility requirement was that the divorce must have occurred before February 15, 1981. The final application date for these benefits was June 22, 1990, although the State Department may waive the deadline in rare situations.

CHAPTER 8

STATE AND LOCAL RETIREMENT SYSTEMS

STATE AND LOCAL RETIREMENT SYSTEMS

T welve million employees of state and local governments are covered by some 2,600 retirement systems. Each state, county, or city sets the rules for pension eligibility and the rights of former spouses under these retirement systems. This chapter provides some general information about how these retirement systems are likely to operate, and it gives you tips on getting information and collecting benefits. It does not discuss specific state or local retirement systems because the plans are so different from each other.

How State and Local Retirement Systems Work

Within a single state, there may be separate retirement systems for state, county, and city employees, teachers, police, and firefighters. On the other hand, several categories of employees may be included under a single retirement system.* A state or local retirement system will normally be based on legislation passed by a state legislature, a city council, or a county commission. A "retirement board" or "board of trustees" is usually responsible for the day-to-day operations of the retirement system. Most state and local employees are required to pay into their retirement systems, though usually not as much as the state or local government is likely to pay in.

Generally, state and local government employees are also covered by social security, but not always.

---

* A large retirement system may be called the "Public Employee Retirement System" (PERS).

Many state and local retirement systems have only limited benefits for spouses and no provisions for *divorced* spouses. However, lawmakers are gradually coming to realize that a wife's contribution to the marriage should be recognized even after the marriage ends. In some states, lawmakers have modelled public employee retirement provisions after federal retirement system protections. But progress has been slow.

Pension Rights of Divorced Wives

Your husband's pension eligibility and your pension rights under a state or local retirement system are likely to depend on state statutes (laws), city or county ordinances, rules issued by a retirement board, or a combination of these. The list of questions in *Part Two* (page 17) suggests the basic information you need to have about his retirement system.

You can probably assume that no benefits from the retirement system are *automatically* available to a divorced spouse. It is likely that you will be able to receive a share of the pension only if you have a court order or property settlement that specifically awards you benefits from your ex-husband's retirement system. Also, there is a good chance that you can only get a share of the benefits your ex-husband would receive, paid to you in the same way (for example, in monthly amounts) and at the same time he is paid.

Special Problems

Trying to get a pension share from a state or local government retirement system can be especially frustrating. If you are dealing with a small retirement system, you may be one of the first ex-wives to try to claim pension benefits in a divorce from that plan. Whatever the size of the retirement system, you may discover that it has few, if any, benefits for an ex-wife, or that the retirement system has no procedures for handling a court order awarding pension benefits to a divorced wife. Plan officials also may be unfamiliar with state divorce laws. These factors can result in tremendous delays and bureaucratic hassles for you.

Here are some problems often encountered by divorcing women when trying to claim benefits from a state or local retirement system and some tips for solving them.

If the tips provided don't help, and retirement system officials insist on being uncooperative, you may have to go to court to enforce your rights. You and your lawyer will have to decide if the time and expense of additional legal action, such as taking the retirement system to court, would be worthwhile.

If You Can't Get Information

Even before you start to figure out what your share of the benefits might be, you may have a problem just getting *information* about how the retirement system works and what your husband's benefits are. Plan officials may not want to tell you about the retirement system rules, at least not without your husband's consent.

If you are having trouble getting information, consider asking a state legislator or city council member (or a member of that person's staff) to help you get a copy of the laws or statutes that govern the retirement system, or at least get you a copy of the plan booklet or other general plan materials. Your state is likely to have a "Freedom of Information Act" which would allow you to get these materials from plan officials.

If no one from the lawmaker's office or the retirement system will mail you information, ask if you can go to the retirement system office and do the copying yourself, or at least go in and look at the material it does have.

If Benefits Are Not "Assignable"

Nearly all retirement systems have a provision that says that a pensioner may not "assign," or sign over to another person, his right to a pension. Some plan officials (and retirees) have argued that this restriction means that they cannot be required to hand over a share of the pension to a former wife. But don't be put off by this objection: Try to persuade your husband or plan officials that this rule doesn't apply to you. In almost every such case that has gone to court, the court has said that the provision against assignment is meant only to protect a pension from the claims of the retiree's creditors (such as a bank where the retiree owes money), not from the former wife.

If the Retirement System Doesn't Provide for Divorced Wives

Retirement system officials may tell you that even if you get a court order awarding you a pension share, they don't have to comply with the order because their retirement system doesn't specifically allow any payments to former spouses. For example, some retirement system officials may say that divorced wives can't collect widows' benefits because a "widow," as defined in the retirement system rules, is a person still *married* to the retiree when he dies.

Your lawyer should find out from those officials what retirement system provisions they are basing their decision on, and then see whether they are correctly understanding the plan. Even if the officials are right about the rules of the retirement system, your lawyer should find out whether there is a state *divorce* law that would help you. For example, there may be a state law that says that pensions of all kinds may be divided at divorce. Or there may be a state law specifically authorizing courts to award widows' pensions to former wives in all cases. It is possible that the state divorce law may let you receive a certain benefit by overruling a restrictive provision of the retirement system.

What Can You Do?

What can you do if none of the applicable laws are in your favor? Many state and local retirement systems still have outdated rules, set years ago before divorce became commonplace, that affect the rights of a spouse. But laws can be changed.

Some ex-wives have successfully launched personal campaigns to get reforms in the law. They have persuaded a legislator or council member to introduce legislation to expand pension protections for divorced spouses. As a result, state divorce laws and state and local retirement system rules have been improving.

If you have trouble getting a pension share, chances are that there are other divorced women who have or will have the same problem with the same retirement system. These women may be glad to join a lobbying effort. You may find that other individuals or groups in your community would also support pension reforms. Organizations in your state, city, or county that may have heard from other women with the same problem, or that may be interested in helping to bring about reforms for divorced spouses, include the state commission on women, the family law section of your state or local bar association, state or area agencies on aging, and retiree and women's organizations.

FEDERAL EMPLOYEES RETIREMENT SYSTEM

The Federal Employees Retirement System (FERS) covers most federal employees hired in 1984 and after, and previously-hired employees who transferred to FERS before 1988. FERS employees earn benefits under the *Basic Annuity Plan* and a voluntary savings plan called the *Thrift Savings Plan*, as well as under social security (*See* Chapter 1).

BASIC ANNUITY PLAN

Similar to CSRS annuity plan, but with smaller benefits.

How It Works. Pays lifetime monthly annuity to retired employees starting at age 62 with 5 years of service (or as early as age 55) depending on employee's year of birth and years of service. A separate supplemental monthly benefit is payable until age 62. Disability retirement is payable at any age after 5 years service. All benefits receive annual cost of living adjustments more limited than CSRS.

Survivor Benefits.

Death Before Retirement. Benefits payable to surviving spouse even if employee dies after leaving government employment but before starting to collect annuity. No cost to employee for survivor benefit.

Surviving spouse receives lump sum or — if employee had 10 or more years service — annuity payable until death or remarriage before age 55.

Lump sum is 50 percent of employee's final yearly pay plus $19,658 (in 1994). Survivor annuity equals 50 percent of basic annuity employee had earned, but is reduced if spouse starts receiving benefit before employee would have reached retirement age.

Death After Retirement. Starting immediately after retiree dies, surviving spouse receives an annuity, payable until her death or remarriage before age 55. Survivor annuity equals 50 percent of retiree's annuity before any reduction. Cost of survivor benefit to employee is an automatic 10 percent reduction in annuity at retirement for the maximum survivor annuity, unless spouse waives all or half of survivor benefit.

A spousal supplement is also payable until surviving spouse reaches age 60.

Transfers from CSRS. An employee with 5 or more years under CSRS who transferred to FERS can receive a FERS annuity, but benefit will be figured like CSRS annuity for years under that system and like FERS for years after. Survivor benefits paid according to FERS rules.

Benefits for Divorced Wives. Former spouse may be awarded a share of annuity through court order. A survivor annuity, lump sum, or supplemental benefit available through court order or voluntary election by retiree. Former spouse may be awarded any part of survivor annuity, unless she waived it while married. Word FERS court orders almost like CSRS orders and send to the Office of Personnel Management. (*See* pages 113-119.)

THRIFT SAVINGS PLAN

How It Works. FERS employee may contribute each year to Thrift Savings Plan (TSP) account up to 10 percent of pay (deducted from paycheck). The government contributes one percent of every employee's pay annually and partially matches employee contributions. (CSRS employee may put up to 5 percent of pay each year in TSP account, but receives no government contributions.) A TSP account includes the employee's and the government's (if any) contributions plus any investment earnings.

In certain cases, such as in financial hardship, an employee may borrow his own contributions. Otherwise, TSP funds may be withdrawn only after employee leaves government. Employee may receive benefits as lump sum, installments over a period of years, or annuity. Funds also may be transferred directly to an IRA. (*See* Chapter 3.)

Survivor Benefits. If employee dies before funds are withdrawn, the money is paid to person he designated as "beneficiary" on special government form. Employee may choose anyone as beneficiary, without notice to or consent of spouse.

FERS employee needs spouse's consent to withdraw TSP funds except as a reduced annuity with widow's benefits. CSRS employee must only *notify* spouse, not get her consent.

Benefits For Divorced Wives. Court order may award former spouse a share of account payable immediately. If the order says you are not to receive your share until later, such as when the employee leaves the government, the order should also award you a survivor annuity in case the employee dies before you receive a share of the account.

The Thrift Savings Plan is run by the Federal Retirement Thrift Investment Board, which has model paragraphs and rules for processing court orders (different from OPM's rules) that award a share of the benefits as marital property, alimony, or child support.

If you are also getting benefits from the Basic Annuity Plan, you should have two separate orders, one for the Basic Annuity Plan and one for the Thrift Savings Plan. Send a certified copy of your "Retirement Benefits Court Order" to:

> Chief, Thrift Savings Plan Service Office
> National Finance Center
> P.O. Box 61500
> New Orleans, LA 70161-1500

For further information, call the TSP Service Office at (504) 255-6000.

INDEX